Rise Gonna Rise

MIMI CONWAY RISE GONNA RISE

A Portrait of Southern Textile Workers

Photographs by Earl Dotter

Anchor Press/Doubleday, Garden City, New York
1979

My deepest thanks to the people of Roanoke Rapids
and to all those who helped with this book.

ISBN: 0-385-13195-X
Library of Congress Catalog Card Number 78–55839

Text Copyright © 1979 by Mary M. Conway
Photographs Copyright © 1979 by Earl Dotter
ALL RIGHTS RESERVED
PRINTED IN THE UNITED STATES OF AMERICA
FIRST EDITION

*To Kell and Cassie,
with love*

*And to the memory of my
mother and father*

Contents

SUNRISE

—song by Si Kahn

Alabama ain't no jubilee
Carolina moon don't shine on me
All over the Southland the changes keep coming
The old ways are crumbling
Like tenant shacks all falling down
They been damming our rivers and tearing up our hills
And wearing down our people
In runaway mills in some town

I got Georgia's old days on my mind
Mississippi magic that I tried to find
You can hear the soft voices of old people talking
They're only dream-walking
The old ways just ain't coming back
And the storm clouds of color are coming together
Like a turn in the weather
Or looking down a long railroad track

Carry me back to old Virginia dreams
Old Kentucky home ain't what it seems
The stone walls of fear that were built to divide us
We're putting 'em behind us
We're finding our hearts are the same
We're growing together and talking out loud
We're strong and we're proud
We're calling each other by name

T for Texas, T for Tennessee
T for trying so hard to be free
But we're talking back now and starting to fight
We're black and we're white
We're children and women and men
And just like at sunrise
We're opening our eyes
You know that we will rise again

Rise Gonna Rise

PART ONE

Victory in Roanoke Rapids

The Day the Union Won

Maurine Hedgepeth, a weaver working third shift at J. P. Stevens' Rosemary Mill, stood at one of the looms she tended. It was just after one o'clock on Wednesday morning, August 28, 1974, the day that three thousand J. P. Stevens workers in seven plants in Roanoke Rapids, North Carolina, were voting for union representation.

Most of the mill workers who came in at eight in the morning for the first shift and those who came in at four in the afternoon for the second shift were asleep now in the darkened town. But night had been blocked out for Maurine by the bricked-in windows and overhead fluorescent lights that created an artificial day in the giant Rosemary weave room. The clatter of looms obliterated the thick stillness of the night outside.

Maurine took a pair of scissors from the big pocket of her striped dress and snipped a tangled knot of yarn. She was singing.

"Gonna roll, gonna roll, gonna roll the union on."

The looms were so loud that Maurine was sure no one could hear her, but her supervisor had. "You sure are happy, Maurine," he said.

Maurine smiled at him.

Then he moved closer. "But you're going to be crying before the day is out."

Maurine looked her boss in the eye. "*You* may be crying today, but I never will."

Down at the Stevens River Mill, on the banks of the Roanoke River flowing swiftly in the darkness, Virginia Davis was warping creels. The fifty-one-year-old mill worker was recalling trouble with the union from her earliest memories.

Her father, Willie Jenkins, had been an overseer in 1934 when mill workers in Roanoke Rapids shut down the plants for three weeks. She remembered the strikers' anger when her father crossed the picket line and went into the mill.

The textile strike was not just in Roanoke Rapids but all over the South. In September 1934 a half million of the nation's three-quarter million textile workers walked off their jobs in the largest general strike in U.S. history to protest low wages, the speed-up of machines, and poor working conditions. Martial law had been declared. National Guard and state troopers swarmed into southern towns to break the strike. Sixteen workers were killed and hundreds more wounded. The strike ended after President Franklin D. Roosevelt promised to set up a textile board to investigate the causes of the strike in return for the union's calling it off. It was not a good bargain. The board broke faith with the President, conditions in the mills continued as before, and fifteen thousand union members were barred from the mills after the strike was lost.

Virginia Davis was worried. Not for herself. Willie Jenkins' daughter certainly was not going to vote for a union, especially when it did not have a chance of winning. But her daughter Shelby Davis Edwards and Shelby's husband, Lewis, were both strong union supporters. Virginia was afraid the company would fire them if the union lost the election. She picked up a bobbin and placed it in the frame of the spinning machine.

In a small cinder-block house about fifty yards from the Stevens Patterson Mill, F. K. Taylor could not sleep. His wife, Lucy, was having a breathing attack, and her coughing and wheezing kept him awake. His wife was retired from the mill now, so he no longer had a personal concern with J. P. Stevens. Still, he could not help but think what the day of the union vote might bring.

His wife's niece Eloise, a frequency checker at the mill, and her husband, Leonard Curtis Wilson, a loom fixer, had been over to the Taylors' house just yesterday. Eloise was saying that Roanoke Rapids would be a ghost town if the union won. Taylor knew how strongly she opposed the union, and he did not for a minute believe that what she said would happen. Still, her words made him think that the fear of unions was still alive in the town.

Taylor lay in the dark remembering that he had been at the J. P. Stevens administration building in 1958 on the day of another union election. He had been governor of the Moose Lodge, and he was trying to raise money for a softball tournament the lodge was sponsoring.

D. C. Turrentine, Jr., the general manager of the Stevens Roanoke Rapids mills, had seen Taylor in the hall and called him into his office. Taylor worked at the state-owned ABC liquor store, and everyone knew that he had a good feel for the mood of the town. He was surprised at how nervous Turrentine seemed.

"Do you think the union is going to win today?"

Taylor thought a moment, then answered, "If they had had an election before all hell broke loose over in Henderson, they would have won. But now"—Taylor shook his head—"people are so scared, there's no way they'll vote for the union today."

Just before the start of the 1958 campaign in Roanoke Rapids, a strike had been called at Harriet & Henderson Yarns, Inc., in Henderson, North Carolina, fifty miles to the west. Harriet & Henderson had refused to renew its contract with the textile union, and the workers had walked off their jobs.

Governor Luther Hodges, who had been a top executive at Fieldcrest Mills, sent state militia and highway troopers into Henderson. The state patrol escorted cars filled with strikebreakers from the Virginia line to the mill gates. The Roanoke Rapids *Daily Herald* had reported fire bombings, beatings, and shootings in Henderson. Then it reported the defeat of the Henderson workers.

F. K. Taylor recollected with no pleasure that he had been right in what he told Turrentine. The Textile Workers Union of America (TWUA) lost the election in Roanoke Rapids that day in 1958.

Harold McIver was exhausted. He had been in the Fabricating Plant, the New Mill, and the Yarn Dye Plant on every shift, talking to the workers about the union. A few days before, a Stevens supervisor had called the workers off the machines to tell them that when the union came into town, strikes and violence followed. The United States Court of Appeals for the Second Circuit found Stevens guilty of contempt while it was under court order to desist from unfair labor practices. As a partial remedy, the court had ordered that a union representative be admitted to the plants to give the workers the union view.

At two-thirty in the morning at the New Mill, across the street from the Stevens administration building, McIver gave a speech in the weave room. He was the southeastern co-ordinator of organization for the AFL-CIO's Industrial Union Department and the man who was running this campaign, which had begun eleven years before, in 1963. The TWUA had lost another election in 1965, but this time, McIver felt, the union was going to win. He knew that the workers were angry about the Stevens profit-sharing plan. Company profits had skyrocketed four hundred per cent, but J. P. Stevens had made no contribution to the employees' invested funds. Stevens had just increased retirement benefits for supervisors, but the workers themselves had no pensions.

Shortly before four in the morning, Maurine Hedgepeth left her looms to work as an official union observer in the election that was soon to begin. National Labor Relations Board representatives, overseeing the voting, sat near the two polling booths that had been set up in the Rosemary Mill cloth room. Maurine watched as the workers filed in to vote.

As the sun came up, James Boone, a twenty-four-year-old black worker and union supporter, met with other election observers at a Labor Board briefing. Later, as department after department of first-shift workers in the Stevens Delta Four Plant where he worked went into the warehouse to vote, Boone had a feeling they were going to win.

Between six-thirty and ten in the morning, workers at the Fabricating Plant voted in the tub-storing room in the shearing department. By five-thirty in the evening, the second shift workers in the River Mill, the New Mill, Patterson, Rosemary, Delta

Four, Fabricating, and the Yarn Dye Plant had folded their ballots and put them in voting boxes. The election was over.

Then the ballots were carried to the Rosemary Conference Room, a small wooden building much like a one-room school-house. The previous Roanoke Rapids mill owners had allowed the workers to store potatoes in the building in the old days. Even now it was known as "the Potato House."

This day the Potato House was filled with eighty folding metal chairs. An aisle down the middle of the room divided them. J. P. Stevens officials sat on the left side of the room, including Turren-tine; A. Edwin Akers, divisional industrial relations director; Tandy Fitts, personnel director of the Roanoke Rapids plants; and William C. Little, Jr., an untitled assistant to J. W. Jelks, Stevens vice-president of industrial relations, up from Stevens' Greenville, South Carolina, southern division headquarters. Union supporters and officials sat on the right side of the room: Nicholas Zonarich, director of organization for the Industrial Union Department of the AFL-CIO; Wilbur Hobby, president of the North Carolina AFL-CIO; Harold McIver, head of the Roanoke Rapids organizing campaign; Cecil Jones, one of the union organizers; and as many of the rank and file union support-ers as could be seated. Many more stood outside on the front lawn.

At the front of the room, National Labor Relations Board rep-resentatives sorted out the ballots that had been carried in boxes from the seven Stevens plants. They counted the votes in piles of fifty. First the "no" votes heaped up, and the Stevens executives smiled. Then the "yes" votes got a taller stack, and the union peo-ple grinned. One pile rose higher, then the other until just before six o'clock. As the last votes were tallied, the "yes" stack stood taller than the "no's."

The Stevens officials looked at the table and got up. They stood in a huddle, then silently walked out of the conference room. When the union supporters waiting outside saw the Stevens exec-utives leave the Potato House by the back door, they whooped and hollered and shouted for joy. The Textile Workers Union of America had won 1,685 out of 3,133 votes, a plurality of 237.

Harold McIver saw some Stevens supervisors, including Wil-liam Johnson, Maurine Hedgepeth's former boss, standing on the porch outside the Potato House. He went over to them and started singing:

> *"Oh, Mr. Bossman, don't you cry for me,*
> *I told you we were going to have a union*
> *And now you see."*

The brand-new textile union members left the Potato House and ran down Roanoke Avenue to their union hall, shouting, "We won. We won. The union's won!"

PART TWO

The Old
Mill Town

Can't Hardly Do It No More

LILLIAN AND LOUIS HARRELL

The textile industry is the bedrock of the southern economy. Its sixteen to eighteen billion dollars in sales annually is thirty to fifty per cent higher than the volume of southern agricultural sales. Textiles account for one quarter of the jobs in five southern states. In North Carolina alone, forty per cent of the labor force works in the mills.

Antiunionism is the bedrock of textiles—the only major U.S. industry that is not organized. Only ten to twelve per cent of textile workers are union members. Textile workers are also the lowest-paid industrial employees in the nation. They bring home sixty-two dollars a week less than the average U.S. factory worker. North Carolina is both the least unionized state and the one with the lowest wages.

Instead of being the end of a long struggle, the 1974 union victory marked Roanoke Rapids as a battleground. Six weeks after the J. P. Stevens workers won union representation, Stevens officials and TWUA representatives went back to the Potato House to negotiate a contract.

The company would not budge on even the most basic proposals. While it was ostensibly bargaining with the union, charges of unfair labor practices were filed against Stevens with the National Labor Relations Board as the textile company harassed and fired union supporters throughout its far-flung chain of plants.

The fight intensified. Both sides entrenched themselves. To

bolster its forces against the textile giant, the 140,000-member TWUA merged on June 3, 1976, with the 360,000-member Amalgamated Clothing Workers of America to form the Amalgamated Clothing and Textile Workers Union. The new union was called ACTWU—which is pronounced "act two."

To protest Stevens' intransigence at the negotiating table in Roanoke Rapids, the textile union, with the backing of the sixteen-million-member AFL-CIO, launched the most extensive boycott ever undertaken by organized labor. The union began a massive organizing drive at Stevens' eighty-three U.S. plants, all but four of them in the South, and J. P. Stevens was charged with bargaining in bad faith with the union.

On December 21, 1977, Administrative Law Judge Bernard Reis issued his finding against Stevens in the NLRB hearings: "The record as a whole indicates that Respondent approached these negotiations with all the tractability and openmindedness of Sherman at the outskirts of Atlanta."

Reis went on to say, "It is elementary that Stevens' efforts since 1963 to repel the union's organizational campaign are founded in basic company policy. The Court of Appeals for the Fifth Circuit stated, 'Stevens has been engaged in a massive multistate campaign to prevent unionization of its Southern plants. . . . The evidence found in the present record fails to dispel [the] impression of corporately designed lawlessness.'

"It can scarcely be doubted that the eyes of all Stevens employees are turned to Roanoke Rapids, the only location at which the union has secured representation rights through an election victory. When Respondent gears up its resistance and actually flaunts its intransigence at the bargaining table as a new weapon in 'its now all too familiar pursuance of full-scale war against unionization,' remedies reaching the length and breadth of its enterprise are imperative."

The confrontation in Roanoke Rapids involves basic premises about textiles and unions, which is why winning is so important to each side. The company and the union are trying to secure millworker support. Both are gambling with memories for very high stakes.

J. P. Stevens and Company, Inc., the nation's second largest textile manufacturer, with 1977 sales of $1.5 billion—is counting

on mill workers remembering that mill owners provided their jobs,
homes, and hospitals in the past. The Amalgamated Clothing and
Textile Workers Union is banking on mill workers forgetting the
repeated defeat of organizing efforts in southern textile mills.

J. P. Stevens could have expected its most loyal employees to be
found among the older white workers who have little or no experience outside the mills, families like Louis Harrell's, who had lived
in the mill town for generations. But memories cut both ways, as
management and union would find out.

The Harrells had been farmers, as Louis Harrell said, "I reckon
since before North Carolina was formed." Louis's paternal grandfather, Edward Harrell, fought in the Confederate Army. After
the Civil War, he tried to farm again but could barely scrape out
a living from the war-devastated land. So, after years of privation,
Edward Harrell trekked with his family to Roanoke Rapids to get
a job at the new mill being built.

In the 1880s and 1890s thousands of impoverished white farming families like the Harrells poured into the burgeoning mill
towns that southern leaders heralded as the salvation of the re-
gion, the foundation on which the New South would rise from
the ashes of the old.

Much of the capital for this venture in cotton manufacturing
came from northern industrialists. Chambers of Commerce in
small southern towns wooed Yankee investors by offering them
tax incentives, virtual control over local government, and "one
hundred per cent Anglo-Saxon, cheap, contented labor."

Unlike many of these southern towns, Roanoke Rapids did not
exist before its mills. From its beginnings, the history of the town
has been the history of the mills, a history of power struggles.

The town was named by John Armstrong Chanler, the New
York millionaire and heir to a part of the Astor fortune, who built
Roanoke Rapids' first mill. When he founded the United Industrial Company in 1895 to spin yarn, Chanler hired his friend the
architect Stanford White to design a mill modeled on ones in
New England. He also contracted with White to construct thirty
houses for the employees.

When Louis Harrell's grandfather came to Roanoke Rapids,
the elegant and eccentric Chanler, dressed in a flowing black cape,
was hammering down loose nails on the boardwalk leading over

Hattie Baker with the portrait of the daughter of the one of the early mill owners.

Two of the seven J. P. Stevens plants in Roanoke Rapids.

Textile worker opening cotton bale.

Three who are fighting for better working conditions in the mills.

Louis Harrell, a retired J. P. Stevens worker, with his grandson Edward.

Kasper Smith with his granddaughter Charlene, after the death of his wife, Irene, a Stevens mill worker.

Maurine Hedgepeth and James Boone.

the mud to his mill. The Harrells witnessed the flamboyant displays of early paternalism, but they were not privy to the machinations of the powerful men who owned the mill they worked in.

After the United Industrial Company had been operating for a year, John Armstrong Chanler, the principal stockholder, received what he considered to be an abusive letter from his younger brother, Winthrop Astor Chanler, the first president of the mill company. The dispute between the brothers that followed was so bitter that John Armstrong changed his name to Chaloner in order to dissociate himself from his brother.

John Armstrong Chaloner told Winthrop to resign the presidency and his membership on the board of directors of the mill company. Then from his Virginia estate, The Merry Mills, Chaloner sent in his proxy to the 1897 shareholders' meeting, voting for himself as president of the United Industrial Company and selecting a board of directors of his own choosing.

A month after the shareholders' meeting, Stanford White, who was also a friend of Winthrop Chanler, urged Chaloner to take an extended rest from business, resign the presidency, and appoint White to the board of directors. Finding business "extremely dull," Chaloner took White's advice and also turned over to him his powers of attorney.

Next, White invited Chaloner to New York "for a plunge in the metropolitan whirl." A few days after Chaloner's arrival at the Hotel Kensington on Fifth Avenue, a physician who had previously accompanied Stanford White on an unannounced visit to The Merry Mills again appeared uninvited at Chaloner's hotel rooms. With the doctor was a professor of nervous diseases, who promptly declared Chaloner insane. Two plainclothes policemen showed up at the hotel with commitment papers, and John Armstrong Chaloner was taken to Bloomingdale, an insane asylum in White Plains, New York.

Chaloner was incarcerated from March 13, 1897, until Thanksgiving eve 1900, when he escaped and fled to Pennsylvania. There, he insisted that a team of neurologists, psychologists, and other physicians examine him. When the doctors unanimously declared him sane, Chaloner returned to The Merry Mills and sent his brother Winthrop a three-word telegram. It read, "WHO'S LOONEY NOW?"

Although Chaloner maintained an active interest in Roanoke Rapids, he did not regain control over the mill. While he was fighting the lunacy laws, the United Industrial Company failed. The paymaster, who was sent from New York to Roanoke Rapids each month with money for the mill workers, had taken the payroll and booked passage to Europe.

After the United Industrial Company went out of business, John Armstrong Chaloner directed much of his energy to the Roanoke Rapids Power Company, in which he also had substantial stock, to fighting the lunacy laws, and to writing about his experiences with the first mill in Roanoke Rapids. His book was called *Robbery Under Law; or, The Battle of the Millionaires*.

Roanoke Rapids' second mill was built by a former Confederate Army major named Thomas Leyburn Emry, who was as much a legend as John Armstrong Chaloner. Emry, orphaned at six, was penniless in his youth. He came from Petersburg, Virginia, to Halifax County, North Carolina, as a tinner when he was seventeen years old. When South Carolina seceded from the Union, he joined the South Carolina volunteers. He was at Fort Sumter during its bombardment and later at Bull Run when the Union Army was routed.

After the war Emry noticed the industrial potentials of the rapids in the Roanoke River and bought up all the land along the riverbank at what is now Roanoke Rapids. Major Emry started the Great Falls Water Power, Manufacturing, and Improvement Company. When John Armstrong Chaloner bought into it, he insisted the name be changed to the Roanoke Rapids Power Company.

Emry built his Roanoke Mills Company on the banks of the river alongside Chaloner's. Before the conversion to electricity thirty years later, both mills were powered by torrents of water directed through giant flumes underneath the buildings. Water wheels connected by belts propelled the looms.

Emry, too, hired Stanford White to design his mill. In the autumn of 1896, blacks picked cotton to clear the land for carpenters hired by Emry to build a second mill village, called New Town, for the 225 employees who made flannels and towels on his spindles and looms.

In 1897 the two mill villages were incorporated as Roanoke

Rapids, and Major Emry was appointed the town's first major. From the start, the mill owners provided all the services in town. The two mill companies hired the town's first two policemen, donated land and money to the new churches in town, and bought baseball bats and mitts for the local players.

In the beginning, Chaloner and Emry stood alone as the powers in Roanoke Rapids. They were succeeded by Samuel Finley Patterson as the symbol of paternalism and prosperity in the town. A member of a wealthy Winston-Salem family, Patterson had been hired by Major Emry as general manager of his Roanoke Mills Company. Patterson, his brother John, and two other investors soon founded their own mill, the Rosemary Manufacturing Company. The largest mill in the area, it produced one third of all the damask tablecloths in the nation. In 1909 a fourth mill company, the Patterson Mill Company, also managed by Samuel Patterson, was incorporated. It made gingham, chambrays, and flannels.

The mill villages, like plantations of the old South, were worlds unto themselves. Ten acres of the ninety owned by the Rosemary Manufacturing Company were set aside for the operatives to garden when they were not spinning cloth. The mill company plowed the land and hired a gardener to oversee the work. Buildings were constructed for canning and storing, including the Potato House.

The mills provided recreation centers, playgrounds, a hospital, and a library. They started a sixteen-piece band and furnished uniforms, instruments, and instruction.

In 1919 Samuel Patterson hired Frank Camp Williams, the man who ultimately succeeded him in heading all the mills in town. Williams was originally hired to play baseball for the Roanoke Mills Company—which had been founded the year he was born. He also worked as a part-time apprentice in the mills for eighteen dollars a week. When the baseball season was over, Williams became the assistant superintendent of one of the mills, and in May 1926, when Samuel Patterson died, he was appointed the general superintendent of the Roanoke Mills Company.

In 1928, when the Simmons Company, the mattress manufacturer, bought all the mills in Roanoke Rapids, Frank Williams became the assistant manager. By 1935 he had become the manager of all the mills, and by 1947 he was president, treasurer, and manager of the consolidated Roanoke, Rosemary, and Patterson Mill companies.

Samuel Patterson had had no limitations on his largesse, for he owned nearly everything in town. And although Frank Williams was a manager and not an owner, he was given a very free hand by the Simmons Company in running Roanoke Rapids. The reality of paternalism remained intact.

When J. P. Stevens bought the Roanoke Rapids mills in 1956, Williams was forced to retire. The company sold the mill houses and recreation centers and withdrew its support from the hospital originally built with funds assessed on tenement property owned by the local industries.

J. P. Stevens had no interest in suffering a cut in its profits by running the mill town with its high overhead costs. The textile company, founded in New England in 1813, had bought the Roanoke Rapids plants to add to the chain of southern mills it had begun acquiring in 1946. When it moved South to take advantage of cheaper labor, Stevens shut down twenty-one mills in northeastern towns.

When J. P. Stevens dismantled the accouterments of the old mill town, it was a jolt to older, white families like the Harrells. Since the first Harrells had come to Roanoke Rapids, whole generations of the family had been born, worked with spindle and loom, and died without knowing life outside the all-embracing mill town. Louis Harrell's maternal grandmother had married an overseer. His father, Henry Louis, started working in the mill when he was seven years old and rose to be a loom fixer. Louis himself was born in one of the company-owned villages.

Louis Harrell started working in the mills in 1928, the year ownership passed into the hands of the Simmons Company. When Stevens bought the mills, the Harrell family worked for them too. With the old system gone, many families like the Harrells were left to shuttle between memories of the old paternalistic way of life and the jarring reality of the new, corporate mode.

I first met Louis Harrell in June 1976, when he was still working, still had enough breath to talk about his plight, before he became a total invalid.

The Harrell's modest home was on a dirt road several hundred feet away from the plastic and neon of the fast-food and motel chains on one of the main thoroughfares. Stanford White's original design for the town had long since been obscured.

Some fifty feet to the right of Louis and Lillian Harrell's house was a trailer where their married daughter, Sarah Bryant, one of their four children, was asleep. She had finished her third-shift work in the mill a few hours before.

Louis Harrell was sixty, with a rugged face and a broad chest. He looked as though he could bellow, but even then the voice coming out of this strong-built man was disconcertingly thin. Louis usually worked first shift as a card fixer, but today he was having one of his bad spells.

Louis had come to the door. Now he eased himself back into his recliner chair. When he was settled, I asked what he first remembered about the mills. He laughed, amused by the question. "They was always there. It all seemed like a natural thing, you know. You'd see it every day. There was nothing new about it. You'd run in and out, go to Mama or go to Papa, if you could find him.

"When we were going to school, we'd stop by the mill and Mama'd tell us where our food was and what to do and to stay out of trouble. Now, my daddy, he'd run me out of the weave room—it's too dangerous—but he'd take me up to other parts of the mill.

"At first it was more or less scary because I was afraid one of those machines would bite me or hit me. That's what they were always telling me: 'Don't put your hand in there. Be careful. It's gonna bite you.' Of course that's the scary part of it. I have seen the time when you could go in there barefooted, no shirt on, go right on through it. You can't go all over like that now.

"All my people were trying to work in the mills, my mama, my papa, my brothers and sisters. We all started too young. Take me. I started working at thirteen and a half. You were supposed to be fourteen, but my older sister Betty changed the records in the family Bible so she could go to work. She changed hers and run me and my sister up one year. I reckon she was afraid they wouldn't believe her at the mill. She was a weaver, worked in the mill all her life, died up here of cancer.

"I worked in the New Mill up until I wasn't quite seventeen. Then I went into the service. The mills at that time were all shutting down. That was the Depression. We had to eat, so I went in the service.

"Then when I was twenty, my father had a heart attack, and I got discharged from the army and came back here to Roanoke Rapids. I didn't go back to the weave room. I went to the card room. Back then, even if you went in there sweeping the floor, you was supposed to be bettering yourself, in your spare time, you know. Not like it is today.

"Well, I went upstairs and ran cards, and then I started fixin' cards." Cards are wire-toothed brushes that disentangle the fibers prior to spinning. "What I do now when I go in is make a round and inspect all those cards in my department. Then I get my tools out and start fixing. Then from that I oil fifty-seven cards. Then I'm supposed to get the lint out. Then I go and do maintenance and overhaul a certain portion of the machines.

"You know carding is the second process of cleaning cotton before it starts being shaped into yarn. There's a lot of dust in the carding room. It beats into a steady fog. Sometimes we have to pull the suction pipes off the cards to see if they're choked up, and that lets more cotton dust in the card room and in our lungs too."

Louis stopped to catch his breath. "But, you know, I can't hardly do it no more. The doctor says, 'We're just going to have to get you out. You can't take this.' And I can't."

Louis handed me a letter from his doctor at the Duke University Medical Center that he had folded in his vest pocket. It said that his "pulmonary problem is exacerbated by markedly dusty environments and this further complicates his cardiac status. We feel it would be beneficial to his health if you removed him from a dusty environment to an environment with cleaner air."

"I carried this letter from the doctor to show them and asked them to find me an easier job out of the carding room. That's the dustiest place in the mill, and that's what hurts your breathing. I showed the bossman the letter, and he told me he'd find me a job as soon as he could. That was over two months ago."

Louis stopped talking as his seven-year-old grandson, Andy Bryant, came out of the bedroom where he had been watching television. The boy, husky and bright-cheeked, was the same age as Louis's father had been when he started working in the mills.

"That boy is going to be a football player," Louis said, giving Andy a hug.

But when Andy sat down and I asked him what he'd like to do when he grew up, he answered, "Work in the mill." Andy said he thought the mills were "nice" and that he wanted to work some in his mama's mill and then in his grandpa's because he wanted to make a lot of money.

After the boy left the room, Louis shook his head. "Ain't that something? He just wants to work there because he thinks I'm a millionaire, and that boy loves money." Louis sat quietly for a few moments. "I give him a quarter nearly every day. That's how he got the idea. I guess we never told him." Andy Bryant did not know that after a lifetime working in the mills, his grandfather made $3.40 an hour.

"When the Simmons Company had the mills, they didn't do you like this. I mean back then we didn't have all these overrated jobs, all these jobs we couldn't handle. Then if a man got sick, they didn't fix it so he couldn't eat. He may have had to take a reduction in pay, but he got a job he could handle. Now, boy, if you can't handle your job, it's 'boom.' When Stephenson took over in 1956, they changed everything."

One constant reminder that J. P. Stevens and Company is an outsider in the old mill town is that most of the mill workers call their employer "Stephenson," a much more common name than "Stevens" in eastern North Carolina.

"When Stephenson come in, the changes in the individual plants were slow, but you could feel the pressure coming down from the top. They didn't put a time-checker on you at first. A nice friendly guy came around and said, 'Could you do that a little faster?' They didn't have a stopwatch, pad, and all that at first, but it got to that. And it wasn't long.

"About the onliest thing that ever slowed them down from pushing us was a couple of times the union come in and try to organize. Now that slowed them right down to a walk. That put them back on their haunches.

"And remember too, another thing. When Stephenson come

in, he promoted all these *real* managers. See, before it was over-
seers. Now they were reasonable people. They were regular people, not men like what they have in there now. They treated men
like people, not cattle. Back then they had some real good supervision. They were mixing with the people, trying to help them.
Now I remember old Frank Williams. He'd cash checks for you,
do a whole lot. The older people especially miss him.

"See, when Stephenson come in here, he got new supervision.
They don't give you no breaks. They're out to break your neck.
I'll tell you the thing that makes me angrier than anything else is
to go to a supervisor and tell him something and have him turn
away from you. You get all nervous and sweaty and don't know
why they won't tell you anything. Now that makes me worse than
angry."

Having abandoned the old paternalistic system, J. P. Stevens
turned to the Human Behavior Institute, now called Behavioral
Systems, Inc., to improve worker-management relations. The
Atlanta-based firm, headed by quarterback Fran Tarkenton, taught
behavior-modification techniques to Stevens supervisors in the
Roanoke Rapids mills.

The institute's 297-page course book *Behavior Management*
recommended "reinforcer menus" and what it called "people priv-
ileges," such as "greeting employees at the door," "departmental
banners," and "pats on the back."

The manual instructed supervisors to "observe how they [the
workers] behave under normal work conditions and you must observe how they behave when you do or say things. You don't have
to take count of these behaviors and graph the number of times
someone smiles. But you should have a general idea how often
this person engages in certain behaviors."

As he talked, Louis had a coughing attack followed by a fright-
eningly difficult time regaining his breath. "My chest feels like it's
gonna bust. And you know how your arm feels when they take
your blood pressure? Well, mine feel exactly like that.

"You know, before I got that hospital bed in my room over
yonder, I used to just go to sleep here sitting up in my chair when
I got so bad I couldn't lie down."

We sat quietly for several minutes until Louis felt better. Then
he told me, "The first time I started having trouble other than a

shortness of breath on a bad day was about seven or eight years ago. Then every time I caught a cold, I got bronchitis and I couldn't get no breath. Then I started to have heart trouble. Then they said I had a breathing problem, and that was what was giving me the heart.

"The mostest thing that bothers me is walking. I've got to where I can't walk far. Yesterday I walked from the parking lot to my job and I had to halt. I've got what they call byssinosis. Brown lung. It comes from breathing cotton dust too long.

"The first time I ever did hear it named was last year when this here Carolina Brown Lung Association set up that health clinic." The CBLA, made up mostly of retired mill workers, was formed in April 1975. One of the association's activities was conducting a series of one-day screening clinics to determine the breathing capacity of participating mill workers.

"They tested me at the clinic and found out I had a 63 per cent breathing capacity. And that's tops for me. I've been tested at the Duke University Medical Center at only 60 per cent.

"You know, back before we heard what was wrong with us, people thought they just had asthma or something. That's what they said about my uncle. He worked in the card room all his life. And he had spells where he couldn't lay down for a week at a time on account of it was so hard for him to get his breath. He got a spell one day, though, and he felt so bad he wanted to lay down. They rested him down on the spinner, and that's where he died. They didn't know nothing about byssinosis in them days."

Although byssinosis has been discussed in medical literature since 1705, the U.S. textile industry successfully blocked research on the disease in this country by refusing access to the mills. Then Dr. Arend Bouhuys, a physician and professor of epidemiology at Yale University Medical School, doing research under a U.S. government grant, tested prison workers in an Atlanta federal penitentiary mill. He found that 29 per cent of them had byssinosis.

In 1967 Dr. Bouhuys published his study, and the following year, with the facts in hand, the U.S. government recognized the disease.

Still the textile industry denied the existence of brown lung. The July 10, 1969, issue of the industry's *Textile Reporter* said that byssinosis was "a thing thought up by venal doctors who attended last year's International Labor Organization (ILO) meetings in Africa where inferior races are bound to be afflicted by new diseases more superior people defeated years ago."

"You know, there are people up in the mill that still thinks brown lung is a made-up thing," Louis said. "There are people in there with it in almost as bad a shape as I am who think I'm putting on so I won't have to work."

Although doctors had certified that he was 100 per cent byssinotic, Harrell, fearing reprisals from J. P. Stevens, was reluctant to put his case before the North Carolina Industrial Commission, which rules on workers' compensation claims. At that time, not a single mill worker with brown lung had received an award from the Industrial Commission.

"I bet you can't find over a hundred people in Roanoke Rapids that's lived to retire. Most of the old people are dead and gone. That's the onliest reason why these unions got in there now. That's what was hurting places like Roanoke Rapids. Too many of the old people, they remembered."

Why didn't Louis just retire now instead of waiting until retirement age?

"You see, Simmons used to give pensions, but Stephenson did away with them when they come in here. What I'm trying to do is hold off retiring till the union can get a pension plan out of Stephenson. You know they're trying to work on that in these contract negotiations. But I don't think I can make it.

"Do you know what Stephenson used to do before the union come in here and tried to straighten him out? Used to be J.P. had something called a profit-sharing plan. One year they'd give you a little bit, and the next year nothing at all.

"How this profit-sharing deal worked was J.P. had some guy up there in New York gambling on the stock market with our money. If he gambled and won, then we won. If he gambled and lost, then we lost. And we didn't know nothing about this fellow. It was like giving your money to a kid. That's why I think a pension plan is better than that setup."

The front door opened as we talked about Louis's possible retirement. It was a major topic of discussion in the Harrell household. Louis's daughter Sarah came in and sat down. She had just waked up and still had on her navy blue slippers. Sarah had short brown hair and a round face.

Did she resent the fact that J. P. Stevens had no pension plan for its workers?

"No. Not really. Mostly I feel angry at him," she said, nodding toward her father. "Because he don't need to stay working now."

Louis stared into the space in front of him. "She just wants me to retire to babysit."

"Not only to babysit. But because," she said, not naming her fear of his dying, "you know. It's just too much on him. He's got four or five flights of steps to walk up at work, and he does that maybe five or ten times every night." Then her voice softened. "And he's a young fellow. It's not worth, you know, waiting for retirement."

Did she worry about getting brown lung herself?

"No. It's sort of like getting cancer from smoking. People don't believe things like that happen to them."

What did she remember about the mills from her childhood?

"Not too much. Sometimes we'd carry Daddy his supper, but you weren't allowed in the mill. But I do know when Simmons had the mills, Mama and Daddy enjoyed working for him. It's different now.

"Mama and Daddy would have preferred that I didn't work in the mill, but there was no other work. Just things like the dime store and those fast-food places."

Sarah was a "sample lady" at the Patterson Mill, making $3.14 an hour. She had worked for J. P. Stevens on and off for eight years. Her husband, Jesse, was in the Navy, out at sea for months at a time. Sarah planned on joining him when his ship returned to base in Norfolk, Virginia.

She also wanted to keep open the option of returning to work in her home town. "If you're union and you quit, you'll not get back in there. That's the problem. I'd like to be able to come back." Turning to her father, Sarah added, "But I'm different from you and Mama. I'm not going to work there my whole life."

What were her thoughts on the union?

"Well, when the union came in, I was scared. There was so much talk about trouble from some of the old people. Even now, some people are union and keeps it to themselves. It's easier on them. Now Daddy won't believe me, but I voted for the union. It's just that I'm one of them that keeps quiet. That's why he calls me a 'scab.'"

Louis had told me earlier, "I hope to God her working up there is only temporary." He wanted Sarah out of the mill. Yet he was vexed that she was not standing with him and other mill workers fighting for their rights.

Why did Louis join the union?

He thought a moment and answered, "The way I figured it, if I belonged to the union and anything comes of it—trouble, you know—I'm too old to suffer much anyway. And if didn't nothing come of it, I hadn't lost anything, I mean nothing more than you're gonna naturally lose if you don't have one. You've got to take a chance on something if you're getting pushed like that. As long as we don't organize, then we'll get pushed around, kicked in the teeth, and everything else.

"I think most of them up there in the mill know we're going to have a battle with Stephenson. Any way you look at it, we're gonna have a war with them. I mean in a boycott. The onliest way we can argue with Stephenson is through the union. I think all the fighting is going to be right here. This is one of the biggest consolidations he's got. I hope and pray we win every darn blame thing we ask for."

Sarah interjected, "The union's slow. They're mighty slow. It's getting bad."

"It's not bad," snapped Louis.

"It's not getting good either. I think that what the people are wanting is for the union to go ahead and do something."

Sarah stopped and thought for a moment. "You know, if they had-a gotten the Teamsters after J. P. Stephenson, J.P. wouldn't be playing dirty ball like this."

"But Stephenson always plays dirty, so what's the difference?"

"What I'm saying, Daddy, is J.P. would have backed down. They would have backed out of it because Mr. J.P. would have ended up in some river in cement if it had been the Teamsters."

Switching arguments midstream, Sarah continued the squabble. "You say they can't break the law, but J.P. breaks the law every day."

"Yes, sir, and they get tried for it every day too."

The Second Circuit Court of Appeals noted that J. P. Stevens had earned "a reputation as the most notorious recidivist in the field of labor law." Stevens has been cited for 1,200 violations of the National Labor Relations Act. Between 1963 and 1976 the National Labor Relations Board found the company guilty in 111 cases of illegal activity. Since January 1977 thirteen additional complaints involving twenty-two individual cases have been brought against Stevens by the NLRB. Reimbursements to workers ordered by these decisions have cost the company $1.3 million, but Stevens apparently still finds it cheaper to pay the price for breaking labor laws than to sign a union contract.

Sarah skirmished with her father awhile longer and then got up. She had to stop by the mill to pick up her paycheck.

Louis turned to me. "Trouble is, people up there in the mill know how bad the situation is, but so many of them have got that damned 'I don't care' attitude about it. Kind of like the way they were about that tax business.

"You see, what they got on their shelves and in their plants, that's what they get taxed for. Well, what Stephenson did was load up his inventory in trucks and park them up and down the road all over. Kinda out of sight. He held them out until the tax men left. It was a great tax dodge.

"And the people in the mill knew they were doing that. They thought maybe they was just slipping a few things by the federal government. There's a little bit of rogue in everybody. They didn't know they were hurting their own selves and the county."

Halifax County, where Roanoke Rapids is located, is one of twenty-two North Carolina counties that received no property tax on $75 million in taxable Stevens inventory from 1968 to 1974 until the scandal was uncovered in the North Carolina press. Sandy Shaw, a tax assessor in Duplin County, quit in protest when the county commissioners refused to press J. P. Stevens for owed taxes. A subsequent investigation by the state revenue department uncovered the secret agreement between J. P. Stevens and Duplin County to appraise the mills' inventory at the 1951 value of the looms alone. In the wake of the disclosures, U. S. Congressman David N. Henderson resigned as the textile company's local attorney and also decided not to run for re-election. And J. P. Stevens paid part of the back taxes it owed, including $382,389.32 to Roanoke Rapids and Halifax County.

After a while, a gray-haired woman in shorts and a shirt came in, carrying two shopping bags. Louis struggled to his feet and took the groceries from his wife, insisting she take the comfort-able chair while he put the food in the kitchen.

Lillian Harrell smiled at the visitor. She had no teeth. They had been pulled long ago after a bout with pellagra. Her legs and arms were marked and bruised from her work, but the wear and tear of her life had not dimmed her warmth, openness, and genu-ine attractiveness.

Lillian grew up in the country, and she still had old-timy ways. "I've been dipping snuff since I was four years old. I love it. I do it at work. I carry me a jar to spit in. About ten years ago they quit setting out cans, so now if you've got to spit, you've got to walk a country mile to do it.

"My grandfather Ed Scott's mama was the first in my family to work in the mills. She used to put her baby in a little box and tie him in there to the framer while she worked so he couldn't get hurt. Yeah, that's the way people used to do.

"All my brothers and sisters worked in the mills, except for one who tied Grandma's apron around her neck and it caught fire. She died.

"I don't even know how I learned to spin, but I did. I sure did. Because I went in there when I wasn't but thirteen to do my mama's job for her while she'd go home and feed the children. My daddy, Herman Scott, was the second hand in the spinning room. When he was a little boy, he was one of those little doffers. Back then, all those little doffers and sweepers would go out of the mill and shoot some marbles and then go back and doff around again. My daddy showed me how to do my mama's spin-ning while she went home. He wouldn't let me get behind. He had to go off and fix, you know, but he'd come back and see that I didn't get all balled up.

"I had learned to spool even before that. My girl friend did it with a bobbin in her hand, and you'd catch that spool thataway and weave it and tie it and hold it and spool." Lillian Harrell leaned forward, animated, and wove her cat's cradle magic in the air. "I learned to do that too. It ain't like it is now. It was different."

As a girl, Lillian had worked in a mill in Smithfield, North Carolina, "on and off until I was eighteen. For about eight years I worked in the cotton mill over in Weldon, and I've been here in these mills near about thirty years now." Lillian was then fifty-six.

"I just hated to see the Simmons people go, because they was good to work for. They didn't do you like Stephenson does. Now, I never did hear tell of *them*. We didn't know who Stephenson was until they got right in here. Then we found out what they were when they started messing with us.

"I was winding when I went to work up there, but they do the spooling on an automatic spooler now. I do winding and spooling in the New Mill on the first shift."

I asked Lillian to describe the spooler frame she worked on.

"It's a long machine and for every frame you put a bobbin in. It's like this," she said, and again her arms and hands moved rapid-fire in a graceful, energetic pantomime of her work, her eyes tensely concentrating on her phantom machine.

"I love to work. But they just about kill you over there now. They're speeding up the machines all the time, stretchin' them out. They're the longest spools in any mill around here. They're like to kill you. I had them hit me a time back."

What about Lillian's breaks at the mill?

"We get half an hour. That's all. At quarter to ten we stop off till ten o'clock. And at quarter to twelve we stop off till twelve o'clock, and that's all we have."

Did her department have a canteen?

"Yeah, but it's down there in the card room about a block away from my work. I'm at this end, and it's at the other end of the room. I'd rather not even go down there. It's too far and it's so crowded you ain't got nowhere to set down. All the menfolks out of the spinning room and carding room is in there, so the women-folks ain't got nowhere to sit. And we ain't got but those fifteen minutes to go to the bathroom and eat our dinner. So you know what I do? I get a cup of water. Yeah, that's what I do. Right out of the spigot.

"We have to stand all day on a cement floor. It's hard on your feet. We've asked them to put some rubber-based tile on the floor, you know, to make it easier on us, but they haven't done it. Used to be they would listen to a white person in the mill, but now they treat the white person like trash."

Had Lillian voted for the union?

"I did and I ain't ashamed of it neither. There might be a lot of things they can do for us. And they wouldn't have got it either if it hadn't been for the colored people. They are the ones that are fighting for it. The white ones are not. I did, but there aren't many of them. Scared of they'll lose their jobs."

Louis returned from the kitchen as Lillian said, "We've been working all our lives in the cotton mills, and you can't take no more. I just wish they'd get somebody up in there that's got some sense to run the mill without trying to push the help to death."

Louis sat down and said what he had said many times before, as though repeating it would give him the strength he needed to carry out his intention. "I'm gonna tell you-all the truth. I'm gonna retire. On Monday I'm gonna start this thing rolling. There ain't no way in the world I can keep on in that mill."

Lillian looked over at Louis. "He says he's gonna quit, but he ain't. It's his life."

The Coffin Maker's House

EULA AND FRANKIE WOOD

Next to the mills, death had been one of the most profitable businesses in town. At the turn of the century, typhoid, malaria, and smallpox were as pervasive as lint. And so the local coffin maker was able to retire early on comfortable savings.

He built a house from lumber salvaged from his shop, with windowpanes fashioned from the viewing glass that covered the upper half of coffins in those days. The small house was near the woods, away from the mill villages where his customers lived. At first it stood alone. But the mills had prospered, and a new village was built on land encompassing the coffin maker's house. Surrounded by mill houses constructed alike and slapdashed with the same color paint, the coffin maker's house was unique.

The Wood sisters, who had lived in the house since 1915, had always been proud of their home's distinctiveness, although today it looked ordinary. In the late fifties, when J. P. Stevens sold the mill houses to the workers, the new homeowners had individualized them, lopping off porches, adding carports and extra rooms. With the backdrop of uniformity gone, the coffin maker's house no longer stood out as it once had. Even its ocher exterior and maroon shutters did not disguise the fact that today it was simply a brightly painted two-story frame house in a modest white neighborhood.

The mill villages no longer existed, and the Wood sisters' neighbors lived in a world which the occupants of the coffin

maker's house did not know very well. They had not kept pace
since they had left the mill.

The two sisters, Eula and Frankie, sat perfectly still in the
corner of the living room that was the dead center of the house.
Their chairs were spaced ten inches apart, and their huddling
made the rest of the neat room look even more lifeless. A print of
a single red rose, Eula's favorite flower, hung on the wall above
the sisters, who kept vigil over the ghosts of the old way of life.

Eula, older than her sister by ten years, hunched in a worn
leatherette La-Z-Boy. Nearly everything about her was concave.
Her thick glasses. The way she carried her body, as though trying
to form a hollow, protected place for herself. Even in her eighty-
first year, Eula had about her the air of a motherless child.

Frankie, as sharp and angular as Eula was curved, jutted her
elbows at right angles to the arms of her hard brown rocker.
Frankie was lean, with a narrow chest and a long face. Whereas
Eula's hair was gray and stringy, cut off severely below her ears
and held back with bobby pins, Frankie's was piled high in a
country-style beehive. A lot of it was still brown. Something about
Frankie was skitterish, snappish.

Eula wore a shapeless housedress and black leather slippers. Her
sister always wore an apron tied over her cotton dress. The room
was silent except for the sound of a vacuum cleaner whirring overhead on the small second floor. The two old women did not look
at each other or at anything in the room.

On the floor between the two sisters, yesterday's paper was
spread to protect the carpet. An empty coffee can and a small
cylindrical tin rested on top of the newspaper. Without looking,
Frankie suddenly reached down and picked up the can. She
brought it to her mouth and spat out a thick stream of reddish
brown tobacco juice. Again without looking, she replaced the can
on the freshly placed newspaper.

Although neither sister moved when the vacuum cleaner
clicked off and footsteps reached the top of the stairs, both sisters
were alert to the sounds. They listened to the metal hose clink
against the banister. They had been waiting for the big dark
woman, with her hair in cornrows hugging her fine scalp, to come
downstairs. She was a highlight in their long, lonely day.

Ernestine Brooks was not a maid. Eula's cataracts and glaucoma classified her as legally blind. The state social services had sent Ernestine for four hours each day to vacuum, grocery-shop, rake the sun-blistered lawn, dust.

Eula Wood also had brown lung, but she got nothing for that. She had been denied workers' compensation by the North Carolina Industrial Commission and the North Carolina Court of Appeals because the law did not cover cases involving exposure to cotton dust prior to 1963.

As Ernestine walked into the living room, the vacuum cleaner still in her hands, Frankie moved to get up from her rocker. "I've got a picture I want to show you." With effort, Frankie pulled herself up and put her weight on her feet. They were flat and more thick blue vein than flesh. She walked slowly, barely lifting her terry-cloth slippers from the floor, and hobbled into the tiny bedroom just on the other side of Eula.

"What's it of, Frankie?" Eula asked in her slow way.

"It's of the bean wagon. I wanted her to see it."

"I think you have some pictures upstairs, Frankie," Eula called out, as though the house were bigger than it was.

Frankie ignored her and rummaged through the top dresser drawer.

"You know where it is?"

"Yeah, I know where it is. You don't think I'd cut it out and then throw it away?"

Eula said nothing as Frankie continued her search. After a few minutes Frankie returned to the living room with a newspaper photograph to show Ernestine. It was of a white-bearded man in a broad-brimmed hat and a loose-fitting suit standing beside a long wooden wagon with shelves instead of siding. The caption of the photograph reprinted from the 1914 Roanoke Rapids *Daily Herald* said that William Strauther was the "bean wagon" man.

"See that house there?" asked Frankie, pointing to a house identical to the ones next to it in the photograph. "That's the house we used to live in when we first moved here, the house before this one."

"There were ten of us come here on the train on August 10, 1910," Eula said. "Mama, Papa, and all us kids. We were barefoot, and that was fine with us. I was fourteen, and Frankie was four. Daddy carried his toolbox, Mama carried the baby, and we had all our belongings in a trunk."

Ernestine took the photograph from Frankie as the old woman eased herself back into her rocker.

"That was a long time ago. You all have seen a lot," Ernestine said. "That's an odd picture with that horse and wagon. I'm telling you it don't look like Roanoke Rapids. I thought Roanoke Rapids always looked like this. What'd this bean wagon man do?"

"He lived over here on the next street," Eula said. "He picked up all the meals and carried them down to the mill. He came along here about nine-thirty in the morning to pick up the basket of food Mama had made."

Ernestine studied the picture of the bean wagon closely. "That thing could hold a heap of good food. I tell you, working there like that must have been better than it is now. I was a spinner up there at the mill for a while, and they didn't even give you time to eat. They just gave you ten to fifteen minutes if all your 'chines were up."

Frankie nodded. "Used to be, way back, you could set down and eat your dinner. Now, it's if you can eat, you can eat. Lord have mercy, they don't give you time to get a drink of water. I'm glad I'm out of there. I haven't been inside the mill since the day I left, and that was in 1949."

"Why did you quit?" Ernestine asked.

"That one who laid me off said I had fallen arches. My health wasn't too good, so they had me quit. They gave me eighty dollars in a lump sum for retirement. See, they didn't have a pension for all of those years I was there. So I got social security because of my health."

"I haven't worked since 1958," Eula said. "When they laid me off at the mill, if my sister and brother-in-law—they were living here then—hadn't let me stay on, I don't know what I would have done. The mill gave me $28.48 a month for retiring, and I had to live off that for two years until I could get my social security."

"They don't care nothing about you when you get old," Frankie said.

Ernestine asked Eula why they had laid her off. "Well, when Stevens took over, they were stretching out the work. You know, giving someone else your job and their own too. They wanted to run it with less help. The bossman said to me that being as I was the only one in my department who could draw that $28.48 retirement, they decided to let me go."

Eula looked more concave than ever, folded into the recesses of her chair. "That time my overseer told me he was letting me go, it was a Thursday. He told me near quitting time, and I just went home. I was hurt, so I didn't say nothing to nobody. That was my last day.

"The bossman told me he'd let me know if he could find any work, so on Sunday night I called him and asked him if they had anything. And he said no, so I didn't call him back no more. I cried for three days. I just set down and cried. But I got over it. I reckon I was the oldest one they let go. I mean, I had been there the longest."

Frankie interrupted her sister. "I was fourteen when I went to work in the mill."

"You mean to say that's all how old you were?" Ernestine asked. "How could they work you up there no bigger than that?"

"I didn't work the full twelve hours. I didn't work but eight hours a day."

"Wasn't that hard on you?" Ernestine asked.

"I had a grand time. I was spinning. But it got harder and harder." Frankie pushed her arms against the rocker and shook her head back and forth. "They work you like dogs."

"How much did you make?"

"I made twelve dollars and a half. I gave my mama the first envelope I ever had. Back then before paychecks, we got our money in envelopes. I gave mine to her till the day I was twenty years old, and that day, Mama gave it back to me. She said, 'Now it's time for you to be keeping it.'"

"See, you've been good. That's why God's blessed you," Ernestine said softly.

"Frankie," Eula said to her sister, "I was working for eight dollars a week. The first money I drawed here in Roanoke Rapids was $5.75. I remember the seventy-five cents part because my daddy said to each of us, 'Now you can have all that's over five dollars.' So I got to keep that seventy-five cents."

Frankie nodded toward Eula and said to Ernestine, "She weren't but ten when she started in the mill."

Eula looked at Ernestine. "That's right. I learned to spin back in the cotton mills in Kinston. We were raised on a farm down there, and that's where I stayed until I had to go to the mill. I didn't like it at all. I thought if I had to stay in that mill, I would die. I was about the youngest one up there. I told the overseer I was older than I was.

"They let us come home for lunch. I'd make like I was sick, and my papa'd say, 'Okay, stay home this evening. Don't go back in until tomorrow.' And so they'd all go back to the mill, and I'd be so happy staying at home."

Frankie looked at her sister, disgusted. "Papa ought to have whupped you."

"As soon as they all left to go back to work, I wasn't sick any more. I had a girl friend who didn't work and we'd have a big old time. She'd take her mama's baby and I'd take my mama's, and we'd walk them in their buggies. The fun was turning your buggy loose."

Frankie looked even more sour and disapproving. She turned to Ernestine. "I was the one in that buggy. I was the baby she was having such a good time with."

"Well, this one time, when Frankie had been real sick with whooping cough, and Mama wanted me to watch her while she worked, I was out walking her with my friend. We were at the top of a big hill, and my girl friend said, 'Turn your baby loose.' And I did."

"Yeah, she stayed out of the mill that day to try and kill me."

"I let her go, and when the buggy got to the bottom of the hill, she fell out. She was like to scream to death. I ran down and got her up and put her back in the carriage. I don't think I even told my mama about it. Well, the next morning, I went back into the mill, and I stayed ever since."

Eula asked Ernestine, "Have you ever heard of 'growing pains'? I used to have leg aches so bad when I first started working. I used to sit down on the side whenever I could and just rub my legs. They hurt real bad from all that standing. That was 'growing pains,' you know. Finally, when I realized I had to stay in there, I just made up my mind. And then I worked. I worked in the mills forty-eight years. See, they didn't make you go to school back then. Now the law makes you, and I think it's a good law. Frankie had the privilege of going to school."

"I hated that school, that old Akers School," Frankie said. "I hardly went much. Now I regret it, but it's too late. What I liked to do was stay home and watch Mama dip snuff. When she'd go out of the room, I'd tiptoe over to the little box she kept it in and take some. Then I'd run out with some in my mouth to the playhouse. By the time I got out there, I was sick as a dog. But I got to like it. Still do."

"Frankie despised that school the way I despised the mill," Eula added.

"I liked the mills," Frankie said defensively. "Work never killed nobody. I didn't know nothing about finery then, and I don't care nothing about finery now because I wasn't raised up to it. The mills is where I got my breeding.

"They had ice cream parties sometimes up in the park, and once a year, Sam Patterson—he owned the mill—closed it down and put us all on the train for an outing. I can see that train good as anything. I mean it was a *passenger* train. It weren't no boxcar. He'd back it off into a little siding over here, and we'd all get on it."

"You mean they'd give you a vacation?" Ernestine asked. "The mill owners?"

"Yeah," Frankie said, "for free. The train took us to Norfolk, and we'd go from there to Ocean View. Sam Patterson had men there with satchels on their shoulders and hands filled with tickets to go on the Ferris wheel and all that."

"It sounds a lot better than what they do now," said Ernestine. "Give you a couple of mean toys for your kids at Christmas. Plastic junk."

"If you're retired, they send you a fruit cake not fit to eat and a ham not fit to eat and a tiny little jar of preserves," Frankie said. "That ham they give you isn't much bigger than your hand, and there ain't no ham to it. And I don't like Spam. I've tried it, but I can't eat it. We give that away.

"Now that Sam Patterson, he treated you right. He wouldn't let *nobody* say nothing about mill people. That was something he didn't like. He used to say, 'You go on and get the lint off you and walk out of here just as nice as everyone else.'

"And he'd give you a ride if he saw you walking up from the mill. He'd tell his chauffeur to stop, and he'd pick you up. He'd say, 'Come on.' And I'd get in, right in back with him. I'd sit there next to him, and he'd ask me how I was getting along. And I'd tell him, 'I'm doing fine.' He'd put me off at the grocery store, and I'd thank him and walk the rest of the way home.

"It seems like so long ago since he died. Used to be you'd have someone to go to. After Sam Patterson died, if anyone mistreated you, you could tell Frank Williams, and he'd do something about it. But then it got so you didn't have no one to talk to if they mistreated you but the Lord. You can always talk to the Lord."

"Way back," Eula said, getting back into the conversation, "we'd stroll up to the depot on Sunday to see the train come in, or we'd walk in Rosemary Park and listen to the band. That was all the recreation we had.

"Sometimes you'd see some things. Once, I remember, there was a man who'd buried himself alive just so people would pay to see it. And another time, an old man came into town with a little monkey. That old monkey. He would just grin. He wasn't bigger than nothing."

Ernestine laughed. "He weren't grinning for nothing. He wanted some money!"

"I worked hard for my nickel," said Eula, frowning. "I weren't going to give it to no monkey."

"It must have been something back then, I declare," Ernestine said. "How did people make it?"

"Not everybody did," said Eula. "I remember seeing a truck carrying off a stove with the fire in it still hot, and that wasn't so many years ago. I never could figure out how they got the stove out of the house with the fire still in it, but I remember seeing it. You see, some mill families couldn't keep up with their payments. It was hard back then. The only reason we made it was because there were so many of us. Papa had all us children work in the mills. We had to, to make ends meet."

"How many of you all were there?" Ernestine asked.

Frankie leaned forward in her rocker and started counting. "Let's see. There was Stella and Carrie. They were Mama's. And

A former Roanoke Rapids mill worker.

Ladies of the Old South.

And the spinners, Eula and Frankie Wood.

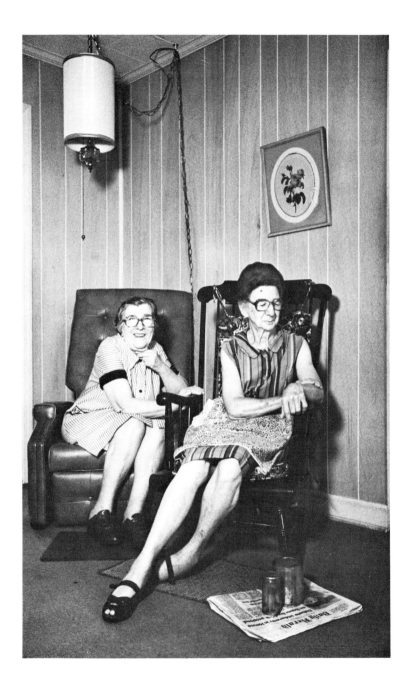

The Masons in Enfield, Halifax County.

Halifax First Baptist Church, open for Thursday evening
Bible study.

Separate and unequal in Halifax County.

"Big Jim" Jones, Ernestine Brooks' father.

Eula and Cy. They were Papa's. Then there was Dollie, Virgil, Lucy, and James.

"See, Eula and me are stepsisters, but we were brought up to call one another sisters. We were taught never to make a difference between us. Her mama died and my mama's first husband died, and so John Wood, Eula's daddy, married Callie Liza Jenkins, my mama.

"Only one time was a difference made between us. One Mother's Day Mama was pinning red roses on all us children. And she had one white one for Eula because her mama was dead. She started to pin it on Eula, and Eula started to cry. Mama said to her, 'Why, honey, I thought maybe you wanted a white rose because your mama is dead.' And Eula said, 'My mama ain't dead!' And Mama hugged her and took the red rose she was going to put on the baby and pinned it on Eula. And she told her, 'I promise you as long as I live, you'll never wear a white rose again.'"

Frankie started counting her brothers and sisters again. "It's hard to remember all of them. So many died. There was one of Mama's twins died of smallpox. Not here but way back yonder in the country. And one of the brothers died of diphtheria in the country. And there was one of our brothers who died when a hammer flipped in his hand and hit his head.

"And Maggie," said Frankie, turning to Eula. "Remember the baby Maggie? She died of yellow chills the year we got here. Then Mama lost another baby that time the cow out back jumped up on her.

"So many died back then. At Bunker's Hill, just across the railroad tracks, they made a pesthouse when the smallpox broke out, and people had to stay out there. What do you call that?" asked Frankie.

"Quarantine. Putting people under quarantine," Ernestine answered.

"Well, anyway, you'd see the wagon going by the house to carry people over to Bunker's Hill," Frankie said. "It's changed altogether now. When we moved here, there weren't but forty families living in Roanoke Rapids. There were only two houses up on the Avenue. This street we live on was called Back Street. Then there was Mill Street. Mill Street folks thought they were better than Back Street folks. There's not many people left from those days. We're the oldest ones from the mills on this block. What didn't move away or die, married," Frankie said.

"We're both old maids," her sister added.

Suddenly a phantom memory overcame Eula—the country smells that had filled her childhood: her mother's wood stove, the barnyard odors from out back, her father's tangy smokehouse.

"We had a cow, chickens, ducks, and geese out yonder." She nodded in the direction of the cramped quarter-acre back yard. "We used to live like country folks. Papa kept hogs way down in the woods—"

"—and killed and dressed them down there," Frankie interrupted. "After he got them cut up, he'd hang them in the smokehouse he used to have out back of the house."

"There was so much work back then," Eula said. "My mama took in boarders and—"

"—she could put up more people than you've ever seen," said Frankie, completing her sister's sentence. "She always kept two big beds in a room. Upstairs there was a girl boarder in with us girls. She worked in the mill too. And in the front room there were four men boarders who worked first shift. Mama did all their washing. Mama and Papa slept right here in the living room. Right over there." Frankie pointed to where a couch stood now.

"We took our bath in a foot tub in here where we had a heater," Eula interjected. "I remember Mama getting the wash-tub out and putting us in it for a Saturday night bath. I was glad when they put the plumbing in. They hadn't got it in too good when Daddy died, and that was back in 1936."

"Mama did all the washing in a boiling pot out back. She done boiled the clothes and scrubbed them on a scrub board, poor thing," Frankie said.

"That must have been so time-consuming," Ernestine said. "But I bet they were pretty-looking clothes."

"That's right," Frankie said. "There ain't nothing like the good Lord's sunshine."

"Mama rinsed those clothes three times. I know because it was my job to go down the street for the water," Eula added. "We each had a job. Taking out the hog slops, building the fire, pumping the water for us and the boarders. I'd get a nickel a week for my jobs, and I was as proud of that five cents as I was of any-thing."

"Miss Eula, my mama used to drink a Pepsi and eat a candy bar and work all day," Ernestine said. "And she used to scrub with that lye soap. Now if I had to do what she did, I'd faint."

"You ain't done work," Frankie snapped at the black woman.

"Like I say, I know I'm right good and smart and hard-working, but I couldn't work like my mama did."

Frankie leaned over and brought the coffee can to her mouth. She let loose a spurt of juice. Then she opened the small tin and wedged a plastic spoon filled with snuff in her cheek. "I'll tell you about working. One time I went to my bossman, and I told him, I said, 'I've got to go and have an operation. I have to be out for a month. Is my job gonna be here when I get back?' He told me, 'Go home, and don't worry. You do what you have to do, and your job will be here.' So I went on to the hospital, and I had both my breasts taken off.

"When I went back to work, I still had bandages, and it was hard to lift my arms to work. But I started doing my job. And my bossman came over to me and said I didn't have my job no more, but I could work helping around. I got angry and said he promised me he'd save me my job.

"There was an overseer named Pendleton, and he was real nice. When I saw him walking by, I give him this." Frankie made a half circle with her arm, an angry get-over-here-right-away gesture. "I told Mr. Pendleton what had happened. He said to me, 'Now you go back and ask your bossman one more time for your job back and talk to him real nice. I'll be back by.'

"So that's what I did. I talked real nice, and he said the same thing he did to me before. Later Pendleton came by, and I told him what happened. He said, 'All right. You just come in tomor-row like regular.'

"The next day, my bossman told me to go back on my job. I never did say nothing to him about it. The day after that, Mr. Pendleton came along again and said, 'How you doing?' and I told him, 'I'm doin' fine.'

"The Lord has been good to us. We're alive and in this house." Then Frankie slowly unbuttoned the front of her cotton dress and slipped it off her shoulders. She took hold of the little ribbon straps of her white slip and pulled on them. The slip tumbled to her waist, and Frankie was exposed: her rib cage like a child's, narrow and well defined; her breastbone prominent.

Where her woman's breasts should have been, Frankie's skin was smooth and taut. Two long scars ran through her breast area to the top of her rib cage. At the base of the scars were two brown spots, her nipples. Frankie sat half-naked. Then, without a word, she pulled up her slip, rebuttoned her dress, and covered her fragile body.

Eula, who had not looked at Frankie, turned to Ernestine and smiled. "She's been blessed, I think. Don't you? She has cancer on her arm too, and she is still here. The Lord has taken care of her. We've both been blessed. I have brown lung and I'm near blind, but I'm still alive. We have this house, and all the rest have left the two of us by ourselves."

Arbutus Drive

RUBY WILLIAMS

Out of view of the mills, near an expanse of pine woods, is Arbutus Drive, a rarefied Roanoke Rapids Eden, with pink roses cascading over the fence running the length of the secluded road. Facing the woods is an imposing residence, the home of Frank Camp Williams' widow.

The welcome mat outside the red-brick, columned house bore the bold red monogram "FCW." Ruby Williams was at her desk in the living room, just finishing up a thank-you note, carefully written on rich ecru paper. Across the hall, in the dining room, sunlight glanced off the exquisite and subtle pale green and silver wallpaper, so like a fine Japanese screen painting. The living room, too, had touches of the Orient—a curved, heavily carved table, some Chinese curios.

Dominating the room were a few magnificent antiques: Ruby Williams' Early American desk, seven feet high, with brass pulls, and the English mahogany breakfront which spanned the entire far wall and housed rare porcelains.

A gilt mirror over the couch reflected the oil portrait of Frank Williams which hung over the fluted mantelpiece. For a house built on manufacturing fabric, the long green couch was indistinctive, its rust velvet pillows not particularly luxurious. The loveliest material was in Ruby Williams' dress—a fine, sheer cotton printed in intricate patterns of russet and navy. Her dress and her living room reflected her own blend of the understated and the elegant. A life built on and apart from the mill town.

Her hair, white in front, dove gray-brown in back, was set soft, old-fashioned, like Ruby Williams herself, the style from a world bygone. She folded her note into its envelope, stubbed out a Tareyton, and pushed her needlepointed chair away from the desk. Today she had already exercised, lunched, napped, finished this letter. She was slightly weary.

"I don't get out much now. I have a crippled leg, and I have to do exercises all morning, every morning. When I'm through, I'm so worn out, I have to lie down. I've been a semi-shut-in for years now, and when I do go uptown, I don't know anyone.

"The old people I knew when I came here in 1921, they'd be about one hundred now if they were living. I guess I am one of the older ones left. The first pioneers, of course, are gone, the Pattersons and all. I guess I am one of the second generation of pioneers.

"I was an R.N. in Richmond, Virginia, before I came here. In those days they didn't have nurses in Roanoke Rapids. They had built the hospital in 1918, but they hadn't graduated a class of nurses yet. So they had to get their nurses from places like Richmond and Norfolk. The doctor called up to the nurses' residence and said he had a patient with appendicitis and wanted a nurse. In those days before we had penicillin, infections often set in. When the doctor called for a nurse, he got me. I was twenty-five at the time.

"I had a date that night and had to break it. I called my boy friend to tell him I was going on a job to Roanoke Rapids. He came to take me to the train, and he said, 'You'd better take a lantern along. I'll bet it's one of those little North Carolina towns.' We laughed. What he meant was that so many of the towns down here then didn't have electricity.

"I got off the train at Weldon and"—Ruby Williams smiled at a remembrance of how things were—"when I got off the train, a young man came up to me and said, 'Are you supposed to go to the hospital?' I didn't have on a uniform, but I suppose they were trained to recognize people. He took me in his poor little broken-down jitney. I asked if it was far. 'Not very far,' he said. It was nighttime, and I couldn't see anything. There were no lights.

"When we got to the hospital, the superintendent told me right away, 'Your patient is one of the mill men.' I had no idea what he was talking about. I didn't know what a mill was.

"The next day I could see where I was. There were no paved streets, except the Avenue. Even there, if you stepped off the blacktop, there were no curbs. It was so muddy and awful. We were always getting our shoes shined. The barber shop had a great business of shoe-shining.

"There was only one little restaurant. People who didn't have their own houses or live in a mill house, all the bachelors, for example, lived in a boarding house and took their meals there. The hospital decided I would stay in my patient's room in the boarding house while he was in the hospital, and that is what I did.

"In the daylight I saw my first mill. I think there were three of them here then. And I could see the mill villages. All of the houses were alike; I believe they were gray. I later learned that the Sam Pattersons built the mill villages.

"The supervisor of the hospital introduced me to my patient. He looked like an old man because he had just had surgery that day. Then the supervisor took me to the chart room, and I looked up my patient's history. It said he was twenty-five years old. So I went to the supervisor and said, 'I've got the wrong patient. This is an old man.' The supervisor assured me it really was my patient, and after a while I got used to the idea. He got better, and after three weeks I took this same little train and went back to Richmond."

Ruby Coffey's patient, her future husband, Frank Williams, recovered fully. "We were married one year after I came to nurse him. When we were first married, we kept that same room and took our meals in the boarding house. Then we lived one block off the Avenue.

"My husband and I started right at the bottom, and we had a hard time with money. We wondered what we spent it on. So we got a little book, and he and I wrote down everything we spent, including shining the shoes. Well, we'd count it up, and we'd see where it went. Nowadays people have everything they want, but back then we just didn't have the money.

"When we were given the opportunity to move, we took it. Really just to get a sidewalk. They had to build the house anyway, so they could just as easily put in a sidewalk also.

"At the time, my husband was just a—really just a worker. I believe he had just become a superintendent at that time. The order went down from Mr. Sam Patterson to build two houses just alike, one uptown and the other downtown. Mr. Patterson said that one was for Williams and the other for the doctor. Still, even at the new house, even with the sidewalk, we had to walk in all that mud if it rained. And when it wasn't muddy, it was dusty.

"What was hardest for me was not so much being in Roanoke Rapids as the fact that I had to sit at home even though we needed the money. In the 1920s women could not work. It was against the law. Married women could not be nurses or teachers.

"I missed my work very much. I hated just sitting, but in those days it was expected that you'd marry and your husband would support you.

"Women—my grandmother and, I'm sure, your great-grandmother—were brought up to be ladies. They spent their time on cultural things. I remember my husband's older sisters. They were over at Meredith College in Raleigh. They'd show you their paintings and the china they'd painted. And you'd wonder how they had time to do all that and their studies. But they weren't educated in academics. It was more for the culture part."

Ruby Williams stopped and thought. "I told you a moment ago that women didn't work in those days. No. I'm wrong. I must be. As I remember it, there were women here working in the mills."

Grande Dame of Lincoln Heights

HATTIE BAKER

Away from the old mill villages, across Chockoyotte Creek to the southwest, just outside the city limits, stands Lincoln Heights. Rows of decaying shanties. Dilapidated outhouses lining the rutted dirt side roads. Some marked with crude, handpainted signs. Others unnamed. A rusted water pump at the end of each.

Hattie Baker lived in one of Lincoln Heights' best houses. It was neat, painted white, her own. A chain-link fence enclosed the small, unlawned yard. She had no bathroom, and although her kitchen had spotless appliances, no water ran from the stainless steel taps. Neighborhood children fetched water for "Miz Hattie" from the pump outside.

Hattie Baker had trouble getting around like she used to. The top of her left shoe had been cut away, revealing several darkened, ingrown toenails. Half of her upper teeth were missing, and some of the lower ones as well.

In one breath the large, rheumy-eyed woman of indeterminate age said she was seventy-five. In the next, she conceded that she was born on "the seventh of December, eighteen-something." Hattie Baker was born in a log cabin alongside the railroad tracks.

Even before Roanoke Rapids itself existed, the railroad had been there, slicing the flat and sandy land of Halifax County. Slaves, hired from plantation owners along the route, had built the eighty-six-mile railroad from Raleigh to Gaston. Later the Raleigh and Gaston Company planned to buy forty-four male and eight female slaves to serve as section repair and maintenance crews and to operate the depots. The scheme for the slave-operated and -maintained railroad was aborted by the Civil War.

From its beginnings, Roanoke Rapids allowed contained communities of blacks to provide services for the white townspeople. The blacks who lived alongside the railroad tracks continued living where they had before the mills were built. Not until later, when the town expanded, were they moved across Chockoyotte Creek into what is now Lincoln Heights.

As a child, Hattie Baker's experience was rural. "We farmed with two oxen, Willie and Dandy. We grew all our vegetables. Mama made her own sausage and all our meal. We made everything except flour. We raised and killed our own hogs. We made soap in Chockoyotte Creek. I remember when the section gang was working on the railroad, people would go up and get the garbage to feed the hogs."

From her vantage point near the Roanoke Junction, Hattie Baker witnessed the beginnings of industrialization in Roanoke Rapids. "I remember seeing the Rosemary Mill being built. That train I lived alongside of brought people to town to work in the mills. They were white, but they didn't have anything. They were kind of junky, you know. They were very poor. We were all poor. The one thing we had plenty of was Jesus.

"These people came from way down South. When the train stopped and these people got off, barefooted and all, my mama used to look at them and say, 'We've got some newcomers.'"

Hattie and her mother closely observed the new mill workers. "Some of them weren't used to colored people. These new people didn't know how to act with the colored. They made you go to the back door. You couldn't sit at the same table with them. Well," Hattie said, folding her arms around her wide waist, her eyes knowing, "if you see one rotten apple, you think they all are."

Although Hattie's family and the other blacks living next to the tracks were kept near-strangers to the new industrialization, they were not entirely unaffected by the mills. "The mill company owned that land we lived on by the tracks. Mr. McMurray was the overseer. Every year everybody who lived on that land had to give him their first bale of cotton to pay the rent. That was the law, you know.

"Until these mill people came in, I didn't know much about white people only except the white Iveys. My Grandma Lizzie told me there weren't a better man in the world than old Dr. Ivey, the man what owned her.

"My Grandma Lizzie's people came over from Africa. She was a genuine Negro," Hattie said with a smile of pure pride. "She met her husband, Elijah, on the Ivey place, and that's where they married. My father was their son.

"After Grandma Lizzie was freed and left the Ivey place, she lived by the railroad tracks. We lived nearby, and she kept me a good amount when I was a small girl. She lived a long time. They say she was 102 when she died."

Hattie Baker remembered something else about her grandmother. "Her arm dropped over on one side so that when she walked, her hand nearly touched the ground. I don't know if it was from slavery times, or an accident, or what. I only know she was always like that when I knew her.

"My mama was Eliza Manley Ivey, and her daddy was Joe Manley. He built the breastworks in that war up in Virginia at Petersburg. It was a war against the Yankees. I don't know *exactly* what it was for. I think it was to free the colored.

"Now my grandpa Joe Manley was mixed with the Indians. He was not *all* Indian, you understand. He wasn't yellow, and he wasn't dark brown either. My mother's mother's name was Mary, and she was part Indian too, but she was not mixed with white people at all." Again that glint of pride. "Both my mama's parents grew up in the Indian section. On my mother's side, one of her back people was the chief Indian. I can't think of his name just now.

"Now I'm talking about that *old* set of Indians, not that young set that lives out there now. Those 'new' Indians wouldn't know anything about me."

Hattie thought again about her ancestors. "I can't remember my grandmother's mama's name, but she was mixed too. That whole gang of them out there at that Indian place was mixed."

Hattie Baker was still a child when her parents moved from the railroad junction to a log house across the creek. "At one time

Mr. J. E. Cox, a white man who was some kind of boss in the mill, owned all that land where we moved to. This land here farther out from town belonged to one man too, Mr. Swindale. He used to own all the land from the big old oak tree that used to stand over there," Hattie said, her eyes following her verbal journey across the raw ground, across the time- and poverty-beaten shanties that those who have persevered here know as home, "all the way back to the creek."

Then she returned to the story of her youth. "My daddy was a preacher. He preached every Gideon chapter. And he farmed some. When he'd go off on revival, Mama and me and my sisters —Minnie, Robena, Mary, and Maggie—would carry on the farm. We never did too much. Just enough to keep us.

"Mama did washing and scrubbing for Miz Dickens, a white lady, and she did laundry for Miz McMurray, whose husband was the overseer for all that land around the junction.

"Before I was even menstruating, Mama'd bring me over to Miz Dickens' and I'd wash the dishes and sweep. When I got bigger, I used to clean house for Miz Hart, and when her daughter, Miz Fannnie, got married, her mama wanted her to take me along with her. So I went with Miz Fannie when she became Mrs. George Hayes. She was the secretary at the Patterson Store, and her husband was the manager. Later, Miz Fannie recommended me to the Sam Pattersons as a cook. I had housecleaned for them some before I started to work for them, and I worked for them for twenty-seven years.

"All of the Pattersons did well. Sam's brother Rufus was a New York multimillionaire. Edward taught at the University of North Carolina. John, Sam's younger brother, was president of all the banks here." He started what is now the Planters Bank of Roanoke Rapids, owned the Patterson Store, and was president of the North Carolina Textile Manufacturers Association during World War I. "And, of course, Sam owned all the mills in Roanoke Rapids.

"The Patterson boys' mother lived in Blowing Rock, and she didn't want them to know that they had anything by way of money. She kept it secret from them, hoping they would do on their own, and they did.

"Sam Patterson had three wives. The first was beautiful. The second was an actress even richer than he was. And the third was Wyche Pearson, the head nurse at the hospital up here. Mr. Patterson said before he married her that he'd marrry him a poor girl who'd appreciate him, and he did. Their daughter, Mary, was born before I went to work for them."

Hattie Baker had a copy of the Chamber of Commerce publication compiled in 1972 for the seventy-fifth anniversary of Roanoke Rapids. She was the only black and the only woman quoted in *A City's Heritage:*

"Hattie put it plain and simple when asked to describe Sam Patterson. 'He was so appreciative over everything. He liked to eat (you could tell from his size) and believed in getting the best of everything. Yet he wasn't choicy; he would eat steaks or pork brains. It didn't matter as long as it was prepared right. Those were the most glorious years of my life.'"

Then Hattie showed off the emblems of her status, the Patterson family pictures that festoon her house: small framed ones of Mr. Sam and Mrs. Patterson, a period photograph painted in pastels of their daughter, Mary, a bonneted child holding a basket of flowers and dressed in a party frock; and photographs, too, of Mary's daughter, Nancy, in wedding white, standing next to a light-skinned black man in formal attire.

"That's my husband, Jimmie," Hattie said. "He's deceased now, but he was the butler. Doesn't he look good enough to be the preacher?"

Hattie had met her husband when he was working for Dr. T. W. M. Long, the Roanoke Mills Company's doctor, and she was working next door for Sam Patterson.

"Mr. Patterson had been sick for a long time. We didn't know what was wrong, but he suffered for thirty years with headaches. He took some kind of medicine that would ease the pain. He had to take to his bed and do business from his bedside."

Hattie remembered May 26, 1926, when "everything stopped in Roanoke Rapids. The mills had already started work that day, and yet the whistle blowed and blowed that morning. People were asking why, and they were told, 'The big boss died today.' They didn't have public mourning for him—" Hattie Baker stopped talking, then added enigmatically, "—because you don't know who your enemies are."

Sam Patterson was building a brick mansion on Roanoke Avenue. "He died before the big house was finished. It took so long to build. There was so much graft and corruption involved in getting all the supplies for the house. The costs had gotten so high they even had to stop construction on it for seven years.

"After Mr. Patterson died, I moved into the big house with Mrs. and Mary. Mr. Patterson had built a brick house in the back for all the servants, but Mrs. Patterson wanted me to sleep in the big house in the room right next to hers.

"I don't know why it was, but Mr. Sam had wanted all white help in the mansion. His chauffeur, Arthur Stowe, was white. He did all the mechanics in the house too. But Mr. Patterson wanted everyone in the house white—the nursemaid, the butler, everyone. Mrs. told him, no matter what, she would never get rid of me.

"Mr. Patterson was already dead when Mary made her debut, you know, when you are finishing up. But I was there." Hattie pressed her lips at the delicious memory. "Hattie Baker was at the Mayflower Hotel in Washington, D.C., yes she was.

"When Mary came out, I was sitting in the balcony with the white servants. I was the only colored there. Mrs. Patterson insisted that I be there. You see, things were a little different back then. It was still Jim Crow days.

"I remember the footman. He was white. He had to stay down there and take all the coats. He came up later when we were watching them all dance, and he said, 'We've got to get up in the morning the same as ever, and they can sleep all day.'

"Well, I looked down on the dancing and didn't say anything, except to myself. And I said, '*I'm* not getting up tomorrow.' I stayed right in the room with Mary and Mrs. Patterson. There were two beds and a trundle that Mrs. Patterson pulled out. I moved it out into the middle of the room. I didn't want them sleeping on top of me.

"They had a kitchen to themselves. Around nine o'clock I heard Mrs. Patterson stirring, and I knew she'd be wanting her coffee same as always. The day after that party, Mary went out around on the town, but Mrs. Patterson stayed in the room, and she wanted me to stay too and talk with her." The grande dame of Lincoln Heights hugged her arms around herself. "I had the best job in the whole United States."

See No Evil

JULIAN ALLSBROOK

The waiting room of State Senator Julian Russell Allsbrook's eight-man law firm on Professional Drive in Roanoke Rapids was stacked high with magazines: *The Tarheel Banker*, *The American Rifleman*, and *Liberty*. *Guideposts'* "Practical Guide to Successful Living" had an article called "They Said I Didn't Have a Prayer." It told of a man much like Allsbrook, a man raised in a mill town who got out of the mills, went to college, and achieved material success.

In his office Senator Allsbrook leaned far back in his swivel chair. His gray hair was combed back, only partly covering his scalp. Behind steel-framed glasses, thin lashes rimmed dull brown eyes. His skin, surprisingly unwrinkled for a man seventy-five years old, was pink tinged. Behind him was a statue of four monkeys—the proverbial see-, hear-, and speak-no-evil figures with hands over eyes, ears, and mouth plus a fourth with its hands covering its crotch.

Julian Allsbrook had been in the North Carolina legislature since 1935, longer than anyone else. Over the years he has advocated the death penalty and backed legislation making it mandatory to teach "the free enterprise system" in North Carolina public high schools, increasing the sentence for armed robbery from thirty years to life, and redefining the "indecent liberties law" to make an "unnatural sex act" a felony rather than a misdemeanor. Senator Allsbrook was also the local counsel to J. P.

Stevens and Company, as he had been counsel to the previous Roanoke Rapids mill owners.

"The mills? Well, my father was the first in our family to work in the mills. He worked in the beaming department in the River Mill. He and his family and my mother and her family had come to town looking for work. Both families had been farmers out in the county. My father got out of the mill and went into the mercantile business. He had various occupations. Later on, he organized the W. C. Allsbrook Company, a grocery store on the corner of Second and Roanoke Avenue.

"When I worked in the mills, we worked a ten-hour day five days a week and five hours on Saturday. And we worked overtime practically every night. And for that we'd draw maybe sixteen or eighteen dollars a week. That was before the minimum wage law.

"You know mill work in those days was right hard, but I really enjoyed working there. Of course, I only worked one summer before school started in Chapel Hill.

"I had a lot of fun. I ran winders up in the cloth room with the superintendent's son. Our job was to take these bolts of cloth from the winders to the table. We had about six or eight ladies we worked with. What they would do was keep up with the winding machines and tack down the bolts of cloth to keep them from unwinding.

"You know, you can make a lot of fun out of work if you will. Whenever the ladies would leave to go out on a little rest or whatever they did"—Allsbrook started to laugh—"then the superintendent's son and me would stay behind and run those machines just as fast as we could, and all that cloth got bunched up. We'd be sitting down waiting for them, and when they came back, they'd fuss with us. We had lots of fun out of them. It was a real happy, fun situation.

"Mr. Sam Patterson? Oh yes, I knew him well. He was one of my best friends. Everyone knew Mr. Patterson. He was a very distinguished person. He had a large automobile with a chauffeur. He was a very large man, immaculate in his dress. He wore spats and carried a gold-headed cane, and when he walked among people, you knew he was there, just from looking at him.

"My personal relationship with him? Well, I mean he knew me

to call me 'Julian,' and I knew him to call him 'Mr. Patterson.' Mr. Patterson was always very warm in his dealings towards me.

"The summer after I worked in the mill, Mr. Patterson called me and gave me a job on his new home. I worked there that summer of 1922 buying local materials for that house of his on the Avenue. It had well over forty rooms. The brick was imported from England, and so was the slate. The costs were enormous. The organ purchased for the home cost about $25,000, and the bedroom had an oil painting by a French artist. It was on the ceiling so they could see it when they were lying in bed.

"Mr. Patterson knew I needed money, so what he did was give me a second job that summer. I was paid $12.50 a week for keeping time at the New Mill warehouse. There was no punch-in during those times. What I would do is go on the job, and the foreman in charge would give me the records saying what time they went on the job."

Was this a created job or was there a problem with absenteeism at the warehouse?

"Mr. Patterson was president and executive officer of the River Mill, the New Mill, and the Patterson Mill, all three. And if he said, 'You're going to keep time over there,' I kept time over there. That was it.

"The last time I really worked so close to Mr. Patterson, he had sent word to me that he wanted to see me. I was at Blue Ridge, the YMCA camp in the western part of the state, and I came back.

"Mr. Patterson said that he wanted the Trinity—that's now Duke University—he wanted their entire baseball team to come down to Roanoke Rapids to play on his team. And he wanted me to be the business manager.

"I told him I wasn't very good at baseball, and he said, 'That's not it. I want you to handle the money and help me.'

"Well, we got the whole Duke team. We didn't deal with the college. We dealt with the individual players. Do you know, the field manager of that team became a North Carolina supreme court judge, and his brother was one of the most famous doctors we've had in North Carolina? We had them, we had them all.

"Mr. Patterson was an ardent baseball enthusiast. He'd just sit right on the players' bench. If they ever lost a game, Mr. Patterson would say, 'Go and get so-and-so on the phone and tell him I'll give him a hundred dollars a week to come here and play.' That was a whale of a lot of money in those days. And we'd bring in extra pitchers, everything like that.

"Something interesting about those baseball games was the rain insurance. Mr. Patterson was great on rain insurance. You could collect four or five hundred dollars each time it rained.

"Mr. Patterson advised the procurement of insurance, and of course whoever the manager was procured it. We went to the mill company's insurance carrier and bought it just like you'd buy life insurance or automobile insurance.

"The rain gauge was set in a garden out there straight across from the Western Union, so the man in there was designated to measure the rain in the vial.

"I was acting under Mr. Patterson's advice, and he told me to go heavy on the insurance. He'd made around a thousand dollars off it the year before. But my year, it would rain enough to keep the crowd away and call the game off, but it wouldn't rain enough to collect the insurance. People paid seventy-five cents or a dollar for a ticket, and when it rained, we would give people tickets for the next game. That's the way it worked.

"I didn't make money off it. I told Mr. Patterson, and he said, 'Don't worry. You keep on. It'll rain.' So I kept on doing it, but we wound up losing. My year, we had a total loss of about four thousand dollars. The ball club lost, but in the long run it was Mr. Patterson because he was the one making up the losses.

"At the end of the season, he called me in because he had some bills to pay. He said, 'Julian, what do you think about trying to collect from the guarantors?' See, we had a bunch of subscribers to the ball club.

"I said, 'Mr. Patterson, how about let's calling it even. Don't you know that anybody who's backing the losing team isn't going to pay off? Now,' I said, 'if we had won, they'd be beating their chests and going around wanting praise. But as it is, the psychology of it is against us.' He said, 'I guess you're right.'

"He said, 'How much money do you need?' I had all the debts with me. And he said, 'Well, now, you add your compensation to it.' I hadn't collected for myself, see. I had been living with my mother and daddy. I had a place to sleep and eat and all, so I said, 'No. There's been a loss.'

"He simply called his secretary and said, 'Give him a check.' He named two accounts. That was the way he wanted to handle it. He said, 'Give him one check for $2,500 and give him another check for $2,500.' So out of that, I think it was a thousand dollars he paid me for the summer's work.

"He told me, 'I deeply appreciate what you did.' I said, 'Well, knowing you as I do, you are a right hard loser. I sense you can't do it and smile.' I said, 'You don't like to lose at anything. That's the reason you've been so successful, Mr. Patterson.' And he said, 'Well, I don't like to lose. I like to put the best that I have into anything and win.' Mr. Patterson was a very determined man.

"I was the business manager for just that season because after I graduated from the University of North Carolina Law School, I started practicing law that October when I turned twenty-one years old.

"My first practice was here in Roanoke Rapids by myself. The mills gave me a retainer. And so for the tremendous sum of one hundred dollars I started out. But the main thing was not the money. They certainly had no need in the textile field for a student who was just out of law school.

"When the treasurer of the mills came up to see me, he said, 'I'll tell you why Mr. Patterson told me to pay you that one hundred dollars.' He said, 'He just wanted to help you, and of course, being a lawyer for an outstanding company adds prestige.' And so," said the senator, "through the mills, I have experienced a lot."

PART THREE

Brown Lung

The Carolina Brown Lung Association Goes to Washington

Cotton Dust Hearings

Eula and Frankie's sixty-two-year-old sister, Lucy Wood Taylor, said good-bye to her husband outside the Carolina Brown Lung Association office, around the corner from the union hall. Taylor rested his palms on the side of the car taking her to Washington, D.C., and said, "Now you be sure to be bad." He smiled and waved as she left, but he was worried. Worried that Lucy might not make it.

Lucy and the others from the CBLA were going to the capital to testify at the Department of Labor's Occupational Safety and Health Administration (OSHA) hearings on establishing a cotton-dust standard. Each chapter of the five-hundred-member Carolina Brown Lung Association was sending a delegation to the hearing. The main contingent, on a chartered bus that had left many hours earlier that day, was making the Piedmont swing through the heaviest concentration of textile mills, picking up brown lung victims from Spartanburg, Columbia, and Greenville, South Carolina, and Greensboro, North Carolina. The people from the Erwin and Roanoke Rapids chapters, in the eastern part of North Carolina, were driving up separately.

Many of them had never been outside the realm of the powerful textile industry. All of them slept fitfully that first night in

Washington, alternately anticipating and dreading what was to come.

On April 26, 1977, the Carolina Brown Lung Association made its national debut when the fifty-member delegation walked into the Departmental Auditorium on Constitution Avenue. For weeks now the room had been filled with well-dressed, high-paid lawyers and lobbyists, medical experts and technicians, each offering testimony on the feasibility of controlling the cotton dust that had already injured countless thousands of mill workers.

No one like the members of the CBLA had come forward to testify in this Chinese green room with its pale gold carpets and draperies, its crafted chandeliers. When the phalanx of old and sick mill workers began their slow procession up the long aisle of supporters, textile industry representatives, and press, all eyes were on them.

Six blinding klieg lights, set up for the three major television networks and a fourth camera, caused some of the brown lung victims to squint as they made their entrance. The cameras whirred and ranged over the lined faces, the two wheelchairs, the denim overalls, the respirator, the two oxygen tanks. The still cameras snapped at the buttons each member of the delegation wore—a large brown one reading, "Cotton Dust Kills," and a smaller yellow one which said, "And It's Killing Me."

The delegation filed into rows of chairs reserved for them up front directly behind the witness table. Judge George A. Fath called the hearing to order, and the opening panel of representatives from local brown lung chapters went up to the witness table.

Lucy Taylor was the first to speak. She showed none of the apprehension that she and the others felt. Her eyes were bright. This was their moment. She nodded confidently to Judge Fath and to the five-member Department of Labor panel sitting at a long wooden table opposite her. She looked out into the crowded room at her fellow CBLA members and smiled warmly at them.

"My name is Lucy Taylor from Roanoke Rapids, North Carolina, and I am proud to be the chairperson of the bi-state board of the Carolina Brown Lung Association. We now have six chapters, three in North Carolina and three in South Carolina. We are a small organization, but we are growing. We want to include as our members every person that has come out of the mills with the chest tightness, the cough, the shortness of breath that is brown lung disease. But we want to do more. We want to do something that will make sure that our organization never gets too big: We want to clean up the dust in the mills.

"We are not technical experts, but we are experts in experience and in telling the truth about our lives. We are sick, but fair and honest."

As Lucy talked, a photographer in a blue jean suit lined in red, white, and blue snapped her picture again and again. Her animated face, her sharp features, her hair the color of an Irish setter, her grandmotherly shape. Someone asked him why he so avidly photographed Lucy Taylor and the other members of the CBLA.

"To show what we're up against," he said. "There are six of us up here from Memphis—the executive vice-president of the National Cotton Council of America, some top staff, us photographers, and the cameraman. We were told yesterday at one o'clock to get on a plane at five o'clock, and here we are.

"We're using stills, color slides, and sixteen-millimeter film. We're going to put together a presentation and show it at the Cotton Growers Association, various board of directors meetings, the National Cotton Council, of course, and to textile manufacturers."

Lucy Taylor, oblivious to her photogenic attraction to the cotton industry, introduced Lacy Wright, one of the first members of the CBLA and president of the Greensboro chapter.

Lacy Wright was seventy-one and lanky. He grew up in a mill village owned by the Cone family and began working in their mill when he was twelve years old, after five and a half years of schooling. He was retired now, disabled with brown lung and on a pension of fourteen dollars a month after forty-nine years of service to the Cones. Lacy buttoned the middle button of his jacket and cleared his throat.

"What I think would be most appropriate would be to give you a little bit of a rundown on what the brown lung organization is and what the aims of it are and what our feelings are as to our relationship to our fellow man and fellow textile workers. Our Lord and Savior told us we are our brothers' keeper, and some way, all my life I have never been able to get away from that.

"If I am my brothers' keeper, and I see people that I work with all my life—I spent forty years in the carding department—and I see people like myself that can't breathe, and I have known them all my life and talked to them, and I hear their problems and I consider their problems, it makes me more aware of how large the job is that we would like to accomplish in the brown lung association.

"Lucy Taylor I think told you that we weren't a very large organization. Now that is talking in numbers. In our feelings, we are a very large organization, and we are a determined organization. I have designated what little life I have left to doing everything that I can to stop brown lung in the textile plants."

In the last row, a National Cotton Council executive sipped a cup of coffee, and listened closely. The Council photographers were still at work as the Spartanburg, South Carolina, delegation went to the witness table. Then the Roanoke Rapids delegation— Otis Edwards, Walter Jones, and Ola Harrell, two black men and a white woman—stepped forward to testify.

Walter Jones spoke first. "I worked at the New Mill thirty-five years. I went in working as a waste picker. Didn't no colored work in the carding department. And I went on from that. They had me as a clean-up man, sweep-up floor man. I run the waste machine, and then I went on as a piece worker.

"I worked as the clean-up man for many years. I used to do weekend cleaning. Every time there was clean-up weekends, I always went back and worked that shift. Then they started to giving us some of these little face masks, and we would use that. But they would get stopped up. That stuff would be banked up there, and it would be pouring down in lumps, and that mask wouldn't last long, so you couldn't breathe air through that. And you just put it down. Sometimes you would have another filter to put in it, and sometimes you wouldn't.

"The cotton on the floor, I'm telling you, was six inches deep sometimes. The whole job that I done for thirty-five years was in the biggest of the dust. You couldn't see across the room. That's just the way it was.

"I just couldn't make it by coughing it up and coughing all the time. I just got so short-winded, I couldn't do the work they were having me do. That dust, it done gone so against me that I seen I couldn't make it no longer, and so that's the reason why I took early retirement. And when I got home, I wasn't no good for nothing."

Then Walter Jones held high a poster with a photograph of Louis Harrell covered with lint. "This is the testimony of Mr. Louis Harrell, who was too sick to come," Walter said to the judge, angling the poster for him to see. As a tape recording began to play, Walter pivoted the poster so that all who were attending the hearing could see. Two of the textile industry men in the last row stood to get a good look. People in the room strained to hear the tape recording of the faint voice.

"My name is Louis Harrell. The last thirteen years I have been having trouble breathing. I seem to be getting worse and worse. I can't lay down and rest without oxygen in the night. My doctor told me not to go back in there under any circumstances.

"They let you quit. They don't try to find you a job, and that shouldn't be that way. They should be bound by some kind of law that if a man works on one job for thirty years, he should get to work for so many hours. There isn't any way in the world that I could start somewhere else and work my way up.

"I think the law or the government or somebody should make a law that if a man has to transfer out of a place because he is sick, he should be given at least pay on a regular basis until he either gets better or retires. He shouldn't be penalized as much as he has to suffer for being sick from the dust thing." The recorder clicked off.

In the last row Gregory Tobin, in a gray suit and dark-framed glasses, the attorney for the American Textile Manufacturers Institute, Inc., took notes on a long yellow legal pad as Ola Harrell, no kin to Louis, began her testimony. "I started working in the mill in Roanoke Rapids during World War II. I worked until 1973, when my doctor told me I couldn't work in the dust and lint any more. I want to tell you about that dust and lint. In the mill I worked in, they blowed off every day. The dust would fly in your face, your eyes, and everywhere. You could taste it. But if you tried to walk away from the blow-off pipes, the boss would tell you to get back on the job, and if you complained about the dust, the bossman would tell you that it wouldn't do you no harm.

"But it did do me harm, and it did do plenty of others harm. And that's why OSHA has to stop the mill companies from blowing the dust in anybody else's face. The mill companies are never going to change unless OSHA makes them change by making stronger rules. And they have got to have more OSHA inspectors too. The way it is now, the mills know ahead of time that company is coming. They get people to come in early on work days and all day on Sundays to clean the mill by the time company gets there.

"Many times I have talked to myself, 'How come I have to work in this mess for eight hours a day, but the same mess is too dirty for visitors to come into for fifteen minutes at a time?' OSHA should come in and see the way the mill looks when the mill isn't expecting them. They should see what it's like. Even in the canteens it's so full of dust and lint that I have to eat my sandwiches in the restroom.

"If the company was willing to clean up the mills, they would have done it by now. The new OSHA rules have to spell out what the company has to do or the mills are going to stay as dirty as they are. The new OSHA rules have to make the mills clean all the time—not just when company is coming."

Otis Edwards, who was sitting next to Ola, started speaking when she finished. He looked at Judge Fath diffidently and said in a soft voice, "I worked in the cotton mill forty-four years. The first fourteen years I worked as a coal roller, and the rest of the time in the dye house, and the last thirty years I worked in the carding room, where the cards are stripped every day. And I didn't have any idea that that dust would injure my health like it did.

"Because if I walked by right now and saw a sign up on the wall, I wouldn't go in. I think that would be a big help if we put some signs up and let the people know how dangerous that dust was. I believe that would help somebody in there. It wouldn't help me because I'm not going back in there."

Then the Greensboro, Columbia, and Greenville chapters came forward, the relentless witnessing of ravaged lives. Allan Poteat from Greensboro, a double amputee, was wheeled to the table. He had to retire in 1970, when he was fifty-two, because of his lungs.

At the time, he still had both his legs. After a car wreck, blood clots developed in his feet, and his doctor told him he lost his legs because his lungs had been so weakened by byssinosis that his heart could not pump enough oxygen to his extremities.

When Poteat first started in the mills, he played on Cone Mills' White Oak baseball team. He was known as "Slugger." After he had worked eight years in the mills, he joined a band based in Greensboro. "The Rhythm Boys" traveled as far as Baltimore. When the group went on the road, Poteat took time off from his mill work. After twelve years on the road, figuring it was time to settle down, he gave up the band, got married, and worked full time in the mill. He worked there a total of thirty-three years. When Poteat retired, Cone Mills did not give him a dime. "They figure I missed it by twenty-one days, is what they told me."

Poteat was conscious of the cameras on him. He pulled his wheelchair closer to the table and looked Judge Fath right in the eye. Poteat, still a showman, was playing for an audience of one.

"I am not going to go into detail, because you have heard here today who the villain is in this case. But I would like to bring up —I'm a veteran, and I was an outpatient in the Veterans Hospital being treated for high blood. And I had an appointment in '70, sometime during '70."

Poteat had a gift for creating the impression of intimacy in a large crowd. He talked in his casual, relaxed way to the judge, as though they were having a chat and everyone else was welcome to listen in. "And the doctor down there said, 'How long has it been since you had an X ray?' You know, they like to keep abreast of everything. I told him, 'A pretty good while,' and he said, 'Well, we'll take an X ray here of you today.' They always take the X ray and say, 'Wait a few months, and we'll let you know how it turned out.'

"Well, my wife and I we were waiting. We come around to a couple of doctors, and they said, 'Mr. Poteat, we have got to admit you have TB.' And they went on to explain to my wife and I that TB wasn't a problem any more, that they could cure it. But they told my wife, 'You can depend on him being here eighteen months.' They said, 'That's how long it takes.'

"So they put me in the hospital, and in the meantime they

started giving me the TB drug, and a couple of weeks later they came by my room one day and said, 'We want to do a lung biopsy on you.' Well, I signed the papers for them to do that. And then they did the lung biopsy, and they come around about three days later and said, 'Mr. Poteat, you don't have TB.' Well, that tickled me. Then they said, 'You've got lung cancer.'

" 'Wait a minute,' I said. 'I'd rather have TB than have lung cancer.' They said, 'Well, we're just telling it like it is.' So there I was, and so then they kept running tests. And then they come back and they said, 'Mr. Poteat, you don't have lung cancer. You've got some kind of fungus, but we don't know what it is.'

"My point in bringing that up is, I have never heard of anybody coming out of the Veterans Hospital and the doctors there telling them they've got brown lung. We all know that we're not going to get no company doctor to tell you you've got brown lung. But surely a federal doctor treating a patient, knowing that you are what you might say federal property, he doesn't have to be afraid of no manufacturer coming down on him."

Other witnesses stepped forward. Judy Kincaid, staff attorney for the North Carolina Public Interest Research Group (PIRG) testified. "In February of 1975 our organization joined with the Textile Workers Union in petitioning the Secretary of Labor to issue a cotton-dust standard. After waiting ten months for a response from the Secretary of Labor, we again joined with the Textile Workers Union, now the Amalgamated Clothing and Textile Workers Union, and filed a civil action in U. S. District Court, District of Columbia, in an attempt to force the Secretary to issue a proposed standard. That was in December of 1975. One year later, in December 1976, the Secretary finally issued the proposed standard that is being addressed today.

"We welcome a chance to comment on that standard. Our remarks today will focus on two main areas. One, that employers not be given seven more years to reduce dust to a level determined safe for workers. And two, that the permissible level of dust should be 0.1 not 0.2 milligrams per cubic meter.

"Let me first address the outrageous proposal that employers be allowed seven more years to implement controls that will reduce dust to a 0.2-milligram level.

"In January 1972 cotton dust was identified as one of five target health hazards by the U. S. Department of Labor. Five years elapsed before the Secretary of Labor issued a proposed standard for exposure. A total of twelve years will elapse before industry under this proposed regulation is required to reduce exposure to a level that is determined safe. We wonder why a health hazard that is a special target because of its severe toxicity should be allowed to cripple workers for twelve more years. The Occupational Safety and Health Administration's answer to this question seems to be that the poor beleaguered textile industry is just not capable of meeting a 0.2 standard within the next year or two years or five years. OSHA seems to be buying the assumption that the textile industry has been trying desperately to reduce its level of cotton dust and just needs more time to reach the 0.2 level.

"We strongly disagree with this characterization of the textile industry. During the summer of 1975 North Carolina PIRG undertook a study of North Carolina's administration of the Occupational Safety and Health Act. The results of our study were published in a report, *Caution: NC OSHA Is Hazardous to Your Health*. PIRG researchers documented numerous examples of blatant disregard for the 1.0-milligram standard that had been in effect for four or five years. In May of 1975 an inspector found dust levels of more than 23 milligrams in a plant where employees were not provided with respirators or any other type of protective equipment. Another May inspection revealed dust levels of 7 milligrams in a plant. In February of that year an inspector found dust levels in another mill up to five times the standard. That plant's superintendent told the inspector that the plant was near the end of its supply of respirators and that he would discontinue giving them to employees when the supply ran out.

"At the time we did our study, only seventeen cotton-dust inspections had been done in North Carolina. As of last Friday, the North Carolina Occupational Safety and Health Administration had completed ninety-three cotton-dust inspections.

"One might think that the more recent inspections would show compliance by those companies with the 1.0-milligram standard. This is not the case. For example, last July inspection of a Cannon Mills plant revealed dust levels up to 3.2 milligrams. This is a time-weighted average. In August an inspector found a time-weighted average of 7.46 milligrams of dust in a Burlington plant.

"These statistics reveal a pattern of negligent and unlawful behavior on the part of the textile industry which disqualifies it from complaining that it needs seven more years to adequately protect the lives of textile workers. We submit that the industry should not be rewarded for its past behavior by a lengthy compliance time.

"The Occupational Safety and Health Act imposes a duty upon the Secretary of Labor to set that standard 'which most adequately assures to the extent feasible, on the basis of the best available evidence, that no employee will suffer material impairment of health or functional capacity, even if such employee has regular exposure to the hazard.' In light of this duty and the available scientific evidence no standard greater than a 0.1-milligram level should be set. Even a 0.1-milligram level compromises worker health for economic reasons.

"Industry representatives argue that it is not technologically feasible to achieve a 0.1-milligram level. Other testimony being presented during this hearing argues persuasively that this is not the case. PIRG has learned that a Gaston, North Carolina, plant has modernized its equipment and is today achieving a dust level of 0.1 to 0.2 milligrams. In any event, OSHA cannot accept some industry representatives' claims about technological disability. It must push the industry into doing what is necessary to reach a cotton-dust level that is considered safe. This standard-setting procedure is a test for the new Democratic administration. Is it going to accept the whining of industry executives, or is it going to roll up its shirt sleeves and use its strength on behalf of this nation's working people?"

Another witness at the hearings was J. Davitt McAteer, an attorney with a Washington-based public-interest law firm, the Center for Law and Social Policy, and author of *Coal Mine Health and Safety: The Case of West Virginia*. "I have reviewed the cotton-dust standard and compared it with the coal-dust standards under the Federal Coal Mine Health and Safety Act of 1969 and the 1972 black lung amendments of that Act. I would like to address my comments where there are direct parallels between the coal-dust standards and the proposed cotton-dust standards.

"The procedure proposed by OSHA that would place the responsibility for monitoring and notifying employees regarding noncompliance in the hands of the employer is the classic case of placing the fox in charge of security at the hen house. Under the coal act, the employer is required to collect the sample and submit these samples themselves to the Secretary of the Interior. The samples are weighed, measured, and analyzed by government experts.

"Given the stringent penalties for violation of the monitoring program under the black lung dust program, the potential for fraud under the brown lung monitoring program, which is under the direct control of the employer, is overwhelming. Unless the monitoring program is conducted and controlled by the U.S. government or some third, neutral party, no employee can have faith in the system, and the possibility that fraudulent data will be forthcoming is very real."

McAteer said that another "glaring deficiency in the standards as proposed is the general lack of education training for both employees and management as to the consequences of breathing cotton dust. Regarding respirators and their use, I believe that this standard is foolish and inequitable because it places the burden on the employee for the failure of actions on the part of the employer. The employees didn't create the dust. They are being injured by it, and now they must suffer because of it. Respirators are simply not worn and for good reasons. They are uncomfortable to wear and to breathe through. After short usage they tend to clog up and cause difficulty in breathing. They eliminate verbal communication, irritate facial tissue, block vision, irritate eyes, and simply don't work. The respirator scheme is clearly unworkable, illogical, unfair to the employees, unfairly advantageous to the employers.

"The proposed rule regarding medical surveillance appear to be drawn from the industrial Dark Age. The hiring of company doctors to conduct a medical examination of employees is a practice considered even by the coal industry as Neanderthal. Even more astounding is a provision which authorizes and empowers the employer to control the medical information on the employee's own medical condition and only be required to give the employees the records of their own examinations on demand.

"The employer, who by having access to all medical information, can review every adverse medical development of each employee and clearly will be in a position to use this medical record as a weapon against his employees, both with information regarding brown lung development and any other illness or injury.

"The medical surveillance scheme is indeed a case of government-backed industrial medical espionage. Any employee who submits himself or herself to such surveillance will be committing economic and employment suicide. When an employee, either because of brown lung or other disease or illness becomes unfit in the eyes of the employer, the employee will either be fired or forced out of work and possibly blackballed from the industry.

"Clearly the employer can be expected to react to this information in a manner best described as 'economic self-interest.' If he expects that the employee might ultimately file a claim for compensation for having contracted such a condition, the employer will in all likelihood fire the employee. The standards proposed here offer no protection against such company tactics. There is no mandatory requirement for relocating such an employee away from the high-dust jobs, nor is there any requirement for maintaining their present salaries."

Charles Hassell, Jr., a Raleigh-based attorney who represents many brown lung victims in their attempt to win workers' compensation, went to the witness table. "Your Honor, during the past two years, it has been my experience to represent persons in compensation proceedings. My clients were employed by the J. P. Stevens Company in Roanoke Rapids, North Carolina, and Burlington Industries in Erwin, North Carolina. In connection with handling their compensation claims, I have inquired of the mills as to what sort of medical information was maintained with regard to pulmonary function studies performed on employees and other aspects of medical surveillance programs that you have heard testimony about during the course of these hearings.

"Among other things, I have learned from my clients, upon receipt of medical reports that were prepared by physicians to whom they were referred by the mills, that in some cases, their lung function was described as being 'severely impaired' and in some cases the medical reports requested that they be transferred, and in some cases the medical reports requested that they not be permitted to work in dusty areas again.

"The point I wish to make is that in several of these cases, my clients informed me that they were *never* informed of the results of their breathing tests, and they were never shown copies of the medical reports that were prepared.

"Most of the people that you have heard testify here today are retired workers. Compensation procedure may adequately take care of some of their medical needs and some of their living expenses. The compensation system doesn't do anything for active workers. Active workers have to be disabled in order to qualify for compensation benefits."

When the last CBLA panel had testified, and the National Cotton Council photographers had snapped their final pictures, the Carolina Brown Lung Association delegation, in a body, left the room. It was not yet time to celebrate. Much still needed to be done.

With Jesse Helms

The next day, the North Carolina chapters of the CBLA went to the Capitol to visit their congressmen. A reception room had been arranged with rows of straight-backed chairs facing a long table for the legislators. The brown lung group turned the chairs to form a semicircle, creating an informal atmosphere. Lucy Taylor walked over to the table and took the center seat. One by one, the North Carolina congressmen came in and sat to the left or right of her. It was clear that she, and not they, was chairing this meeting.

Lucy introduced her fellow CBLA members, and they spoke. Then she laid it on the line: She asked each legislator if he would work for the brown lung legislation that Senator Ernest Hollings had just promised the South Carolina chapters of the CBLA he would introduce. The CBLA wanted to know who was for it and who against. To underscore the point, Lucy added in her rasping voice, "If we didn't have confidence in you, you wouldn't be here."

Just as she said this, North Carolina's senior senator, Jesse Helms, appeared at the door and, as unobtrusively as possible, took a chair in the back of the room. Lucy Taylor, as alert a politician as Helms, spotted him. He was the one she wanted.

On the national level, Helms was a leader of the conservative wing of the Republican party. He was the Reagan backer largely responsible for that candidate's victory in the 1976 North Carolina presidential primary. Facing stiff competition for his Senate seat in the upcoming election year, Helms would have liked to avoid being on the line in so controversial an issue as brown lung legislation. Because Helms got his start as a radio announcer in Roanoke Rapids and maintains a vacation home nearby, he was well known in the area.

"There's a seat for you up here, right by me, Senator Helms," Lucy Taylor said. "We're awful glad you could be here. Come on up."

Reluctantly Helms made his way through the curve of chairs, edged past Allan Poteat's wheelchair, and took a seat with Lucy and his colleagues. Ola Harrell opened her purse and pulled out a handful of CBLA buttons to hand to each legislator. Senator Helms pinned his directly beneath his enamel pin of the American and North Carolina flags. The others followed suit.

Then he addressed the group. "Now I have been in the midst of suffering. I have a sister who had two brain-tumor operations. But I can say to those of you here who spent your lives making and building an industry, we will have to find some help.

"I think I can speak for the delegation in regard to Senator Hollings' bill. I want to say that we will carefully scrutinize it, and we will see how it can best be handled, whether by state or federal legislation.

"You did the right thing coming up here. There are a lot of doors to money up here. Now don't be discouraged if one of these avenues doesn't work. There are lots of avenues. We will take whatever action is deemed proper to take, whether on the state or federal level. We will work to try to get relief for these people who have worked for so many years and have excessive medical expenses.

"Now I have just come from the Senate floor, where they are trying to give aid to North Vietnam. It's ironic the way priorities work in this country. That people like you who have built our country, who have never asked for a handout, are forced to spend a lot of time getting around technicalities to get compensation, while the U. S. Senate is trying to give aid to the Communists.

My recommendation is that we keep the money here for people like you."

On his way out of the meeting, Helms was stopped by a Charlotte, North Carolina, television reporter. Yes, he had time for an interview for the evening news. He put an arm around Lucy Taylor and stood before the camera. "In all candor, extreme care must be exercised in connection with any brown lung legislation. I must say that this is fraught with complexity. But the bottom line is that we've got to arrive at some help for these people."

Helms kept Lucy in his embrace when it was her turn to speak. Lucy said, "The people have suffered for so long. Now I think we will get some help, which I think is wonderful. We've known them for a long time, and they have promised to help."

The moment was recorded. The camera turned off. Helms walked away. Lucy Taylor was left standing there. Her exhaustion was beginning to show. The newscaster noticed and said sympathetically, "You must be tired."

Lucy nodded in assent, put her hand on her chest and said, "Talk, talk, talk."

The Fight Isn't Over Yet

On their third and last morning in Washington, the CBLA delegation paid a call on Dr. Eula Bingham, the head of the Occupational Safety and Health Administration. Fourteen brown lung victims sat at the long conference table that filled the royal blue room. The rest of the fifty CBLA members and staff were in chairs against the walls, under oil portraits of seven Secretaries of Labor.

Promptly at eight-thirty Dr. Bingham walked in and took a seat between Otis Edwards and Walter Jones. She assumed correctly that the association knew the sullied seven-year history of OSHA, this agency which so affected their lives.

Some OSHA scandals were uncovered in material subpoenaed during the Watergate hearings. George Guenther, who had headed OSHA during part of the Nixon administration, promised, in a confidential memo in answer to Nixon's appeal for "responsiveness" on the part of government agencies to his re-election campaign, that "no highly controversial standard (i.e. cotton dust) will be proposed through November 1972 as part of the program to promote the advantages of four more years of properly managed OSHA for use in the campaign."

Dr. Bingham, who had been appointed by President Carter six weeks before, folded her hands on the table in front of her. "The past sins of this agency at least were not committed by me. So I think I'll just say I cannot be held accountable."

She looked around the room at these people who had the courage to speak up to judges, senators, and administrators, sick people who had used their strength to demand that injustice be righted. "I need *your* help," Dr. Bingham said. "I need all the help I can get. Sometimes it seems like the only people who will come here are the people who own the mills and their lawyers. It is very difficult for me to get people in government to understand that we're talking about a rule or regulation that deals with people."

Then she did something that none of the senators or congressmen even came close to: Her eyes filled, and her bottom lip quivered. She tried to go on. "Some people don't understand that." She was crying and could not go on. "You all must have things you want to say."

Essie Briggs from Columbia, South Carolina, rose to the occasion. She stood and said, "I've worked in the mills ever since I was eleven years old. I had to retire because of my lungs." Then she stopped to wipe her eyes. It was happening to all of them. Lucy Taylor fought back tears. Some of the men blew their noses.

In the presence of Dr. Bingham, the pent-up emotions that had been held back during the testifying and politicking were released. Through her own touched feelings, the woman who headed the government agency responsible for their health shared with these disabled mill workers the impact of their own lives, the fearsome, cruel, and inhumane reality of what had happened to them. Nearly everyone in the room was crying in these last shared moments in Washington.

Just as it was nearing the unbearable, that old showman Allan Poteat came through. A question floated across his face. He turned to Dr. Bingham. "Where you from?" he asked, breaking the mood but not the intimacy.

"I'm from Kentucky, from tobacca country." She had said "to-bacco" with an unmistakable flat *a* on the end. Poteat heard it and nodded approvingly. They both smiled. Allan Poteat had gotten them composed again.

Dr. Bingham spoke seriously. "I think the fight isn't over yet. There is no question but we have to have a law to regulate cotton dust in the mills. I hope we do not have to be sued to follow through with it. We will select a level that, hopefully, will protect people. I'm not sure how low it ought to be. I will tell you I would like to see the law go into effect tomorrow. I think that seven years is an impossibility. It just cannot take that long."

The delegation broke out into applause, but Dr. Bingham had more to say. "It may be necessary to put a regulation out that would allow people to transfer at the same pay rate of their last job. I think we will have to have 'rate retention' as a regulation all its own. Some people tell us that it is illegal, but we are going to test it. But we don't want to put it in a package with cotton dust, because if we are sued, we don't want the standard held up."

Again she spoke to the association members as equals in understanding the complexities involved in reaching a solution that worked. "You know as well as I do there is a great deal of pressure. We are honestly having a little family fight right over at the Department of Agriculture because they have people telling them they'll get out of the cotton business if we go ahead with this standard. But we are going to hold the line as far as we can."

Dr. Bingham told the CBLA members that it was her turn to testify. She had been called to appear before the House Government Operations Subcommittee to explain why it takes so long to promulgate OSHA standards for dangerous workplace substances. The General Accounting Office had already testified that at the current rate, it would take OSHA more than a century to establish needed standards just for the substances already identified as hazards.

After Dr. Bingham left to keep the appointment in her own race against time and the bureaucracy, Allan Poteat turned to his wife, Naomi, who was standing by his wheelchair. "Boy, I wouldn't have her job for nothing."

Outside the Department of Labor building, Lucy Taylor and others from Roanoke Rapids and Erwin said good-bye to the

South Carolina and Greensboro contingents. Lucy climbed on the bus and said to the driver, "Take care of this crowd. They haven't got their compensation yet." The Greyhound bus with "In Touch with America" on the door pulled away and headed back on the highways going south, back to cotton country.

They Just Wanted to Stand Up for Their Rights

F. K. AND LUCY TAYLOR

Outside the dark green cinder-block house near the Patterson Mill, an Irish setter barked at the stopping car. Inside her four-room house Lucy Taylor was resting. Two of her grandchildren, visiting on their way home from school, were in the living room using her CB radio.

The youngest child was in the back yard playing alone. His siblings would not let him near the CB. They said he was too little. But he had a "handle" like they did. Everyone called him "Buster Brown" instead of John.

"Puppy Dog" had "Bad Man" on channel 18. He had a voice as wispy as hers. "Are you a buffalo or a beaver?"

Puppy Dog didn't understand the jargon. She tried to think of an answer.

"Tin Soldier" slumped in Lucy's rocking chair, waiting for his sister to give up her turn at the radio.

"Are you a boy or a girl?"

"A girl."

Bad Man had already told her he was ten. "How old are you?"

"Nine," Puppy Dog said.

Tin Soldier was fed up. He got up from the chair and went into the bedroom where Lucy was lying down.

"Grandma, tell her to quit hogging that line. There could be an emergency."

"There's *going* to be an emergency here right now if you don't stop. Now you both go outside and play."

Puppy Dog put down the mike and headed for the door, her brother behind her.

Lucy called out to them. "Before you go, come here and let me give you a hug."

Both children kissed their grandmother, then went out to play in the yard with Buster Brown.

"Sometimes they get on your nerves, you know, when you're not feeling so good, but I love them to death," Lucy said, coming out to the living room in her beige mules and knee-length cotton robe. She sat down in her upholstered rocker. The air conditioner was on high, as it almost always was, to make it easier for Lucy to breathe.

"I'm on that CB all the time when the children aren't. I don't talk much, but I listen. I like to put it on at shift change and kind of keep up with what's going on at the mill. I like to hear what people are griping about coming and going to work."

A picture of Christ hung above the small bookcase filled with an encyclopedia set. The CB was next to a Bible on the veneer end table beside Lucy. Several copies of *Labor Unity*, the Amalgamated Clothing and Textile Workers Union newspaper, lay on the coffee table in front of her.

Like her sister Frankie, she had had cancer. Years ago she had her left breast removed. Like Eula, Lucy was suffering from brown lung after a work life in the dust of the mills.

She had just gotten out of the hospital. She had returned from the cotton-dust hearings exhausted and had had to go for total rest, for oxygen, and to use the Byrd machine, which helped break up the congestion in her lungs.

"I wore all my brown lung pins when I was in the hospital, the ones we wore in Washington. I had them all over my nightgown. Those girls in Respiratory Therapy just loved them. They'd tell me, 'Keep it up. Just keep on pushing.'

"There are a couple of them who are not from here. One's from over in Scotland Neck, where they don't have any mills. She said

she's never worked in a hospital where there are so many people
with lung trouble as here in Roanoke Rapids.

"Taylor sent me over a beautiful orchid. I wouldn't take off my
pins even for that. I put the corsage on my pillow and kept all my
pins on. Cecil Jones called from the union hall, and Lillian Harrell, Louis's wife, came by. A lot of people I talk to on the CB
stopped in. See, we have a roll call so that the CBers can check
up on the ones who are sick. When I didn't answer the roll call,
a couple of them came to the hospital to check on 'Lady Irish
Setter.' That's my handle. 'Mr. Clean' came and 'The Praying
Man.' It was fun meeting him after talking to him so much.

"I'll tell you who else came by. My minister, Marvin Faile,
from over at the First Baptist Church. He's Senator Allsbrook's
minister too. He asked me if there was anything he could do for
me, and I told him, 'Yes, pray that I get my workers' compensation.' I felt like adding, 'and I'd like two folding chairs,' but I
decided for once to be a lady and not to say anything." Lucy
laughed and then explained. "Before we had an office or anything,
when we were having our first brown lung meeting, we wanted to
borrow two chairs, and he wouldn't loan them to us. None of the
churches would.

"You've met Eula and Frankie. I have another sister, Dollie
Riddle. She's got brown lung too. Dollie and I were over at the
hospital at the same time. She was on one floor, and I was on the
other. Her daughter Eloise and Eloise's husband, Curtis Wilson,
came to see both of us. Those two are in with that stupid bunch,
that J. P. Stevens Educational Committee crowd that's trying to
get rid of the union. They were both on 'Sixty Minutes.' She was
the one who had her head peeking around at the camera."

When she first retired from the mill, Lucy lived pretty much as
her sisters did, within the confines of her own home, watching
television. Then one day she saw Ralph Nader on a television
forum talking about byssinosis, which he called "white lung" back
in the days before it became commonly known as brown lung.
Nader described the symptoms: tightness in the chest, a cough,
and shortness of breath.

Lucy thought to herself, "That's what I have," and when
Taylor came home from work, she told him about what Nader
had said.

Not long after that, Lucy spotted an ad in the Roanoke Rapids *Daily Herald* asking people who thought they had the symptoms of the disease to clip out a coupon and send in their name and address. Although she suspected it was a gimmick, Lucy sent in her name. And when brown lung organizers—who had already established CBLA chapters in Greensboro and Columbia—came by to tell her about plans to set up a one-day screening clinic to test mill workers in Roanoke Rapids, Lucy offered to help.

After her minister refused to lend the chairs, Lucy turned to a friend who ran the Myrick School of Dancing. Margie Myrick agreed to let the CBLA use her studio for the clinic.

After the clinic was over, Lucy Taylor and Louis Harrell helped start the Roanoke Rapids chapter of the organization. Louis was the chapter's first secretary, and Lucy became president. Later she was elected state president and then bi-state chairperson of the whole organization.

She had always been an organizer. She was born gregarious. Even as a child, of all the Wood children, Lucy was the one whose chores took her out of the coffin maker's house and into the neighborhood the most. "At that time," Lucy recalled, "when it wasn't against the law for people to have pigs in the city limits, neighbors would save scraps for Daddy's hogs. I'd go around and get the slop. I had a bucket and a little wooden red wagon that my father made for me. I started doing it when I was six, and I would do it every day. My daddy gave me a quarter a week for my chores.

"People would make candy and cookies, and I'd stop and talk with them. Everybody had something for me, and I'd be having a good time until I'd see my daddy coming for me. Then I'd fly up the street and get home.

"Another job I had was going to the store for people that didn't have children, the old people. They would give me a nickel for that. Then when I was nine, I started working downtown at B. Marks' store. I only worked on Saturdays—in the shoe department—because I had to go to school, but I think I made about a dollar for the day. I always worked, and I always had my own money. I couldn't tell you when I began working in the mill. I started going in when I was six and first went to school.

"Now, I never saw my father work. He was way down in the

River Mill. In fact, sometimes he would work two or three days at a stretch when something would break down at the mill, and I wouldn't see him at all.

"My mother worked in the New Mill after I started in school. The other kids and I would cut through on our way home. We'd go in one door and out the other, just to wave at someone we knew. I started going in there because I wanted to be with my mother, to help her so she wouldn't be so tired. She was a spooler, and they worked long hours, like twelve hours a day or something.

"She knew I came in there to see her. I would tell her to take a rest and let me do it some. I'd take the thing she had on her hand to tie knots, and I'd get all the ends tied up real fast because I was so young and spry. I'd get done real fast, and I'd go over and talk with her, hang on her neck. I probably made her more tired.

"I didn't really start working myself in the mills till I was four-teen. Then after school let out, I went in and worked some hours. I'd go in and work any place they needed me. I think I must have gone into the spooling room first. A lot of children worked like that, you know. I didn't have to do it every day. I mean, I just did it when I wanted to, but most of the time I worked every day. I think school let out at two-thirty, and I'd work from then until about six. Then I'd go home and do my chores.

"It's funny when you get to thinking about those things—it just didn't seem like work. You had a good time. You laughed and talked with other people. I think that one of the reasons I wanted to work in the mill was that each mill had its own softball team, and I wanted to play. When I went to work in the New Mill, we had games against the other mills.

"At one time, we had a real good baseball team here too. We had a big baseball park and everything. They hired players back then who didn't have to work in the mills at all. They were called the Roanoke Rapids Jays, and they played other cities.

"Thinking back on it, it just seems like a fairy tale turned into a horror story. When I think about the way they are doing the peo-ple now, it makes your heart ache."

Like her sisters, Lucy Wood Taylor's life is rooted in her days in the coffin maker's house. "I loved that house. It's hard to ex-plain, but we had a wonderful time back then. When we went to play at someone's house, either my mother went with us or we played at the house of good friends of hers. The children that came to our house were friends. I mean, you didn't just run up and down outside everywhere like a wild thing, you know. We played in the woods a lot too. We'd do things like look for holly for Christmastime.

"I remember the silent movies. That was the fun of Saturday. Everyone went to the matinee. You could go to the movies for a dime, buy a bag of popcorn for a nickel, and a bag of peanuts and a drink. That would be your quarter.

"Everybody in the audience read out loud. They were mostly children. And the Crutchfield girl was down in front playing the piano. All the children loved her and tried to sit down there in those front-row seats. I think that children could read better then because of silent movies. Whoever was sitting next to me would read, 'Hands up, you dirty so-and-so.' I'd say it out loud too. Everyone in there was reading it out loud, so if there were children in there who couldn't read, they would learn from everyone else.

"I loved school, all of it. I loved it because it was a crowd, and lessons were no problem. I was a smart person in school. I had so many certificates for perfect attendance. I didn't ever miss a day. In the middle of the first year, I was promoted to the second grade, and then I got promoted to the third grade and then on up to the fourth.

"I must have been a little hellion. I looked like a little old anything. It didn't matter to me if my clothes matched because when the report cards came in, I would be on the honor roll. I had always talked about being a lawyer. My teachers knew I had the potential.

"It's funny, but I never thought of myself as living in a mill village, though I suppose I did. The houses all around us were mill houses. My husband says that in some towns, mill people were called 'cotton-mill trash.' Well, I guess maybe they were here too, but as far as we were concerned, we didn't ever hear it.

"Now when I was a child, I did hear older people talk about people who moved here from other places. They were people who had moved off a farm and gotten a job in the mill. I don't know where they came from. People who had lived here all of their lives would say those people were more or less trash. But, I mean, people wouldn't say they were 'cotton-mill trash.'

"They were people who didn't care about how they looked or what they did. They would get out in the yard and raise Cain and use profanity in front of the children. As a child, you just didn't hear that sort of thing. My older people would say about these new people, 'Don't go down to their house.'

"Some of the mill workers had terrible, terrible lives, but it wasn't because of the work. It was because their husbands drank or something like that. Like the lady who lived next door to us. She had all those little children, and her husband drank and threw his money away. He wasn't much good. My mother used to give them milk and butter.

"I could look down from my bedroom window upstairs into her house, those two houses were so close together. The woman was very sick. One time I saw old Dr. Long go in."

Lucy interrupted her story. "Did you know Dr. Long delivered me? I'm named after his nurse, Lucy Hyman. My niece Eloise was named after a mill company nurse too. Back then so many people named their little boys after Dr. Thomas Williams Mason Long."

She continued. "Dr. Long made out a prescription and left money for it there on the mantel. Well, the next day he came back and found her husband laying down and the money for the medicine still on the mantelpiece.

"Dr. Long picked that man up off the bed and shook him and told him he had just so long to get down to the corner drugstore and get that medicine. See, the doctors loved you then. They would take care of you.

"Some time after that, one of the little boys from next door hollered for me to come to the window. I went to see what he wanted, and he said, 'My mama's dead.' I looked over, and I could see through the window where she was lying right there on the bed with nothing to cover her face.

"Back then families looked out for one another more than they do now. Families were a lot closer then than they are now. I don't know what happened. I only know life has changed. Have you noticed it?

"I know a man who works in the mill who lives next door to his mother and father. At some point, his parents put up a fence around their house. Then later the son and his wife got mad at the father, so they put up another fence. Now there are two fences separating the son from his parents. That's the way people can be. They change.

"I didn't grow up knowing class. People wouldn't talk about that like they do now. As a child, we played together. I went to school with Mary Patterson, Sam Patterson's daughter. We took violin lessons together. I remember their cook, Hattie Baker, and the chauffeur, Mr. Stowe. He would pick her up from my house or take me home from hers.

"At home, we kids made our kites out of newspaper. One time I was at Mary's house, and she asked her mother for money to buy her a kite. Her mother was in the bedroom, and she called out to us not to take more than a nickel for her and a nickel for me. I said I had already made my kite, so she told Mary just to get a nickel for herself and then get me to teach her how to make a kite like mine.

"You know, it just seemed like I had a very happy childhood. I just don't remember not being happy. People seemed to love one another more then. People cared, and everybody knew everybody else.

"Another thing I don't understand is when the hate started. I never grew up with it. You know, my mother had a colored woman who helped her. She'd be at our house when Mama was working in the mill. This colored woman's name was Pat Simmons. She had a daughter, Elizabeth, who is four months older than me, from August to December. Pat brought her daughter over while she worked. We called her Doll Baby. After her mother died, she came over here and worked with me. She lives over in 'colored town.' I guess they call it Lincoln Heights now.

"Pat's family and a lot of the other colored used to live down by the cemetery. They had a right hard time. People didn't pay them much. If Pat didn't get to work some, they just didn't have food. She'd come by our house, and my mother would give her what she had.

"Most of the colored lived over the river in Gaston or in Northampton County. I remember when they didn't allow colored people in the city limits after dark. I remember that unless a colored person worked for you and lived in, they couldn't be around. People used to fix up a little place for them to sleep. I know my mother set up a cot on the porch for the colored people.

"The blacks you had in your house never went to town. I don't think anybody sent the people that worked for them on errands. If they needed something, they sent their children. You'd never see colored people walking on the streets of Roanoke Rapids, but I don't know why. Maybe because they had such a hard time. Maybe that's one of the reasons they wouldn't let them into town late. Maybe they were afraid some of them would steal or something.

"I do know that this little girl was killed over in Halifax. The family had a colored man working around the place. He had worked there all the child's life. They claimed the man did it, and they hung him, the white people did. They just left him hanging and made all the colored people go look at him.

"I don't even know when they could stay out past sundown. I do know that they had a Ku Klux Klan here when I was a child. I never saw them or heard it talked about at home. I don't even know when it ended.

"They seemed more humble then, colored people. I can't remember a time when they weren't in my home. I can't remember being taught hate—I mean, thinking, 'You're black, and I'm white.' I just don't remember that part of my life.

"I just can't remember when people got to hating each other. It seems so strange. I have to sit here so much, you'd think I'd think about things like that. When I have the family over here now, Doll Baby is right here with us. We all hold hands to say grace, you know. She holds hands with the rest of us. We had a picture taken of her right in with the crowd. I think at that time I had two pictures, and I gave her one. Then when Doll Baby's mother died, we sent a wreath of flowers over there.

"I just wonder why all this mess started, all this racial mess." Lucy rubbed her throat. "I guess they just wanted to stand up for their rights like maybe the South against the North. The South wanted to keep it the way it was, and the North wanted to free them. Or—" Another idea came to Lucy. "Maybe they're like mill workers standing up for their rights. I hadn't thought of it like that."

Lucy was solemn, but suddenly her face brightened. Taylor was home from work. He had strong-built shoulders, close-cut white hair, and a wonderful twinkle in his eye. He was sixty years old, two years younger than his wife.

"Taylor's a big union man, and he doesn't care who knows it. Right, Taylor? See that name on the mailbox outside, 'F. K. Taylor'? We tell people, 'When you come in here, leave J.P. at the door.' 'F.K.' is for 'Ford Kemp,' but no one calls him that. Before we were married, I called him 'Mr. Taylor.' When we got married, I dropped the 'mister.' "

Taylor sat down and said, "I was born in the shade of a cotton mill. My father died when I was a baby in that 1917 flu epidemic. I have a picture of him coming around the mill with a big old sack of waste cotton on his back. From the time I was four or five, I'd go up the block to play outside the cotton mill. There was cotton lint strewn from the doors and windows from fifty to a hundred yards. My whole childhood I made wagons out of the old cog-wheels from the spinning frames they'd throw away. I used picker sticks for bats and shuttles as cars we played with on little roads we made in the sand.

"This was in Catawba County, in the western part of the state. I grew up in Newton. It has cotton mills and silk mills, but it's not a mill town. They had furniture factories there too.

"I worked in the silk plant in town for five years, starting when I was sixteen for thirty-two cents an hour. We made so little that I never did hear tell of people paying income tax until 1941. My oldest brother was a weaver. I filled magazines for him. I did some weaving too.

"Later I worked in the cotton mill in Cherryville nearby, running combers in the card room. But I only stayed six months. I couldn't stand a cotton mill. When I first started there, I had to work three weeks sweeping up. I would get a three-by-six-by-four-foot-deep box full of lint from the floors every two hours. My nose would itch and burn. Everyone said, 'Oh, you'll get used to that.' But I thought, 'Good God Almighty, if I have to stay and do this the rest of my life, I'd rather die now.' I told my bossman, 'If this is all you've got for me, I'll go.' I told him, 'I believe I'm one of the best.'

"After that I drove a cab for a while, then I sold insurance, and then I started working for the ABC. I'm the manager of their largest store in the county.

"You know," Taylor said, looking over at Lucy, "we've been knowing what she's got all our lives. I remember as a kid talking to people with their heads stuck out the windows trying to get a breath of fresh air. That was before they bricked up all the mills.

"My sister died at forty of lung trouble, and her husband at fifty-seven. They both worked around cotton. My brother left the mill at thirty-three with lung trouble. He had a heart attack when he was fifty-four and was totally disabled. All the people my brother worked with are dead.

"Long around when I was young, we called what they got 'cotton mill crud.' The rich people called it consumption. What they didn't tell you is what we were consuming was cotton dust.

"I'm no doctor, but I can recognize brown lung from a block away. I've been looking at it for fifty years. The last seventeen years of our lives have been filled with hospital stays, waiting in emergency rooms, trips to the doctors and drug stores, and the everlasting coughing.

"When Lucy was up in the hospital, the other patients complained because they couldn't sleep. We've bought cough syrup of all kinds by the bucketful. I guess she must have had at least a fifty-gallon bottleful. She's coughed thousands of times to my one, and I was smoking four packs of cigarettes a day.

"For the last ten or fifteen years, she's coughed every night. Half the time she gets me up with her coughing. Then when she gets quiet, I start to worry that she's dead. I've gone to bed a thousand times like that, half the night sleepless because of her coughing, and the other half worried that she's died. Never a night passes that I don't look and see if she's breathing.

"After I go to sleep—and it takes right much to wake me up—I wake with a start when I realize I don't hear her breathing in my dreams. I've been doing it for years. I take naps now in the afternoon to make up for the sleep.

"I've seen her cough for twenty-four hours straight, and it gets me so nervous. We finally had to sleep in separate beds so I could sleep at all. I am thinking of suing J. P. Stevens for 'alienation of affection.' There are hundreds of people all over town the same way.

"She used to be on the phone all the time with her sisters. We finally had the phone taken out and got this CB. Her breathing couldn't stand all that telephone talk. She can't grocery shop or anything any more. I have to put her in the hospital at least three or four times a year.

"It's gotten so I don't know at what point I should make her go to the hospital or just wait and let her make the decision. They can't do anything to cure her, but when she goes, she gets her lungs cleaned out, and she gets some relief. But I could turn around and put her back in as soon as she comes out, her breathing is so bad all the time. When I go to work, I call my daughter to have her come over and check on Lucy during the day. I thank God my daughter has never seen the inside of a cotton mill.

"I know why I don't like cotton mills—the way they treat their help by threats of shutdowns, three-day work, moving out, firing people, and making them sick. I believe the southern textile workers will organize and stand up for their rights.

"Lucy is really something with this brown lung organization. I don't know how she gets up and talks in front of a thousand people the way she does. I worry about her, she gets so tired. But she's a battler. She'll battle me, and anyone who'll do that won't back down. She and all of them in that organization are real fighters."

PART FOUR

Civil Rights

Once You Be Down Low

ERNESTINE BROOKS

Across the bridge over the Roanoke River, one mile out into Northampton County, Gaston is perched on a hill. The town is little more than a crossroads: C&W Sporting Goods; the M&M Supermarket; the Gaston Drive-In Theater, separated by a corrugated iron fence from the neighboring cornfields.

Down the hill, back in Roanoke Rapids, the J. P. Stevens River Mill sprawls on the riverbank, strikingly industrial in contrast to Gaston, where old black men in overalls sat outside the M&M watching cars pass by.

Farther out on the sandy, dry land, four miles from Roanoke Rapids, two miles from the Virginia state line, Ernestine Brooks, back from work, was in a small wood house on a dirt road, her in-laws' house. A car passed, stirring up the gritty road. The dust permeated the house, settled on the gold plaster cupids, the picture of Christ. Ernestine was telling Clarence and Hazel Brooks about the Wood sisters and the coffin maker's house.

"I had no idea those old white ladies had it so hard coming up. They got no education, and they started working twelve hours a day at ten years old. I never heard that whites had it like that."

Clarence Brooks, in a battered hard hat, listened to his son's wife. He knew plenty about those mills. He had started working in them when he was fifteen, back in the thirties, baling cotton forty hours a week, making $12.32, walking ten miles back to the old farm in the middle of the night, working days on the land.

Clarence Brooks had *heard* of Sam Patterson, but he hadn't ever actually *seen* him. And he didn't know Frank Williams. But Brooks had his own stories, his own memories of the history of the mills to tell the white woman who had come to visit with Ernestine.

"You ever hear tell of the flood we had here in 1940? They started letting us off work when the water started coming up to about here." Brooks measured a few inches above his ankle. "The next day I had to go back. I was going in to get my check, and I waded in water up to here." This time he marked off a place on his thigh. "Well, I got over there and I couldn't get back. The water was clean smooth across the bridge. Whole bales were floating down the river, from *both* sides of the mill.

"When the water started going down again, we had to start cleaning up the mill. We had to take a shot every day to work in all that water. We hauled all the cotton that was left up to the New Mill. There was wet, heavy cotton everywhere. That's what I remember most about the mills."

"That's one thing about Roanoke Rapids that I don't care about is those mills," Ernestine said. "My first impression of them was a prison. No windows. They got you shut in with brick. They got you closed in with ear plugs."

"Shut in. That's right. You can't see out," her father-in-law added.

"I worked for Stevens in 1971 or 1972 in the Rosemary number-three spinning room," Ernestine continued. "To tell you the truth, when I first went in there, I thought I had stepped into hell. I thought I knew what hard work was, but until I went in there, I didn't.

"Those spinning frames is the most ridiculous-looking things I have ever seen. They are the meanest-looking contraptions. One frame is the length of a large house trailer, and I had twenty-six of them to take care of. They have them hopped up as fast as you can hop them up, and all night long you walk around and around them, looking for threads that are broken."

"Those spools go so fast, they're gone with the wind," Clarence said.

"I would imagine, going two laps I walked a mile around them," Ernestine added. "I walked until my feet about fell off.

They told me, 'You can't wear cheap shoes up here,' so I bought an expensive pair for $19.95, and still my feet hurt.

"Whenever you found a broken thread, and you found them all the time, you had to hand it up, the end of the thread, and make it catch on the bobbin. Like on a thousand gigantic sewing machines. I thought these spinning contraptions were a mess because if you didn't catch the thread just right, it would burn you.

"My bossman told me, 'If you don't get your 'chines right, then you don't eat. You'll just have to swallow fast.' They wouldn't even let you go to the bathroom when I was there. When I asked my bossman if I could go, he said I couldn't leave my machines. I asked him what I was supposed to do, and he said he didn't know. He said he couldn't help it, that I couldn't leave. 'Unless you're smart enough to keep all those machines going, you can't go to the bathroom.' I got almost crazy in that job. To tell you the truth, it got on my nerves.

"It was a stinking job. I got paid minimum wage. Two dollars and something. I worked there about six months. My supervisor told me, 'You'd better do a good job and you'd better not quit because you won't get another job.' I asked him why, and he told me, 'Because we need a spinner.'

"They expect humans to keep up with machines. You can't do it unless you have magic go-go. They just run them machines day and night, night and day, clack-clack, clack-clack, all the time.

"When I left Stevens, I went to the Kentucky Fried Chicken on Tenth Street. I fried chickens for sixty-nine dollars a week after take out. Later I went over there to work at Eula's."

While her husband and daughter-in-law talked about the mills, Hazel Brooks cut out a dress pattern and listened. She had on a white blouse, plain skirt, and a print kerchief. She knew nothing about J. P. Stevens or Roanoke Rapids. "I've been on the farm most all my life. Just in the last few years we had to come off. They've got so many machines now, they don't need labor any more. That's what the man we always worked for told us. So we had to move from there down here. Now we don't farm at all. I miss it.

"We used to work corn, cotton, and peanuts. We had to shake the peanuts by hand. Now they've got the equipment to shake them. The man we worked for used to bring some of his cotton down to Roanoke Rapids and sell it, but he doesn't gin any more. He used to bring wood down to the paper mill by mules and wagon. He'd cut down the pulpwood and skin it first. You could get a better price that way. They didn't have machines do it then. He doesn't do that any more either."

Ernestine looked admiringly at her mother-in-law. "She's smart. She knows how to do a lot. She's the one who taught me everything."

Ernestine explained that she herself had been a city girl. She had come down from Richmond to visit an uncle who lived on the white man's farm where the Brooks family sharecropped. There Ernestine met Clarence junior when she was fifteen and he was twenty. "We got married because we were just so much in love and half crazy.

"I had never worked in the fields before," she continued. "When I started, everyone said, 'Poor thing, she ain't never seen cotton before. She don't know what to do with it.' At first I always cut up my fingers. The cotton, you know, comes first in green little squares, and you have to learn how to pull out that cotton without ripping your fingers all apart. It's an art, too, picking cotton.

"When I first went out in the fields, people were working and toting, with the hot sun beaming down all day. I thought they'd never want to stop and drink some water. But you know how it is with older people in the country, they are watching you all the time. So I'd heave up that hoe, and they'd watch. I'd heave it and heave it. It would take me the longest time to make a big hole.

"Now I can go and chop a hole in a minute. Clarence's mother can chop a hole like nothing you've ever seen. Country people have been doing this stuff all their lives. I think I've come a long way. I can clean hog chitlings, plant a garden. Not as good as her" —Ernestine nodded at her mother-in-law—"but good. I believe I could even make lye soap if I had to. I believe I can do anything if I put my mind to it.

"After we were first married, we lived with Clarence's family. Then we moved to a little bitty place with no bathroom. I didn't like it at all. It was way back in the woods two miles from the road. For a city girl, it seemed like forever from the highway. That's what bothered me the most. Everywhere you looked, there

was nothing but a whole lot of darkness, and a whole lot of bull-
frogs and crickets and hogs.

"I was pregnant. I had a baby every year. I didn't like that time
in my life at all. To tell you the truth, I went into the woodwork
back then. I weren't doing no work outside the home. I was just
taking care of my babies. Then in 1966, after I had my fifth
daughter, they started giving black ladies the pill, the IUD, and
such at the family planning center."

Ernestine's husband, Clarence junior, walked in. He was thirty-
six and sinewy. He had just gotten off work on a construction job
in Hopewell, Virginia.

"It's a union job. They pay him $5.45 an hour. They won't pay
that kind of money around here," Ernestine said. "But it's an hour
and a half drive each way every day, and I think that's too much
time. But over in Virginia, it's much better. Wages, welfare, everything. In North Carolina, you're just paid the worst, the very
lowest. At first I didn't realize it.

"Like when I first saw Roanoke Rapids after I'd been here a
long while, it looked pretty good to me. When you're used to
being on the farm with chickens and cows, and then you see lights
and shops and all that, it looks mighty good, but then you get
used to it. Right now I'd say, to me, Roanoke Rapids is one of the
lowest towns there is."

Ernestine glanced at her husband. "He's a very hard worker.
One time, he cut and loaded four truckloads of pulpwood all by
himself in one day. I think he deserves credit for that. I think that
should be written about. Tell her about it, Clarence."

Clarence, shyer than his wife, did not look up when he spoke.
"I was twenty-six years old when I did it. The truckloads were five
feet by five feet. The wood itself was of different thicknesses, so
that one truckload weighed fourteen thousand pounds and another weighed sixteen thousand pounds. The four trucks averaged
out to fifteen thousand pounds apiece.

"The man paid me a dollar for cutting and loading each thousand pounds of wood. I'd load up a truck, and the man who
owned the wood would drive the truck away. Then he'd bring it
back and I'd load it with more wood I cut. I worked like that by
myself all day. I cut the wood by a chain saw with my own
power."

Ernestine interrupted Clarence. "Can you imagine that? With no one to help him, cutting and carrying about fifty trees on his shoulder for each truckload?"

"It didn't bother me."

"I look at him sometimes, and I think, 'Lord have mercy, I don't know what got into him that day.'" Ernestine shook her head with a mixture of admiration and sadness. "I think my tongue would just be hanging out full dead if I had to do that."

"It ain't bad. I had decided I *had* to make some money that day, to try to get ahead. If a man laid back any, he couldn't have done it. He had to be willing all the way to do a job like that, but I wouldn't do it no more.

"Why? Because I've got more noggins now. Because you can't do that to your human body. That's one machine you can't overhaul."

"A human person should not have to do that to make a living," Ernestine added. "You know what I want to do? I want to take a three-month course at the Halifax Community College and learn to be a nurse's aide. I love to serve people, to help people. That was born in me. I like to feel like I am accomplishing something.

"The school says it places you in a job after you finish the course. I just hope I can get a job working in a hospital to support myself and help my husband. The way I figure it, by helping ourselves, we are helping our children.

"If you are limited in education, it's hard to come up. Once you be down low, it's hard to work your way up, to rise up even just a little bit. But I'm willing to try to see if I can make it. I'm willing to see if I can go a little further, I'll always do my best."

Colored People
Weren't More Than a Dog

LUCY AND OTIS EDWARDS

In Lincoln Heights men were standing downwind of the smolder from a burning truck tire, warming their backs and hands against the cold, not far from Lucy and Otis Edwards' house. The shivering men were within a hundred feet of the charred ruins of a house where two old women had died a few weeks earlier, and on the corner of the road where two children had burned to death in a fire several days before. Five tires sat at the edge of the Edwardses' front lawn, like symbols of prosperity. They were not burning; they were painted white and served as planters for Lucy's greenery.

Opposite the Edwards house, identical wooden shanties were propped up on cinder blocks, like oversized matchboxes. Each had a sorry outhouse behind it. The Edwards house, like Hattie Baker's two roads up, was white. It had freshly painted green aluminum shutters. On the front porch, red metal lawn chairs held promise of summertime leisure.

In their cozy living room, Otis Edwards proudly displayed the latest issue of *Brown Lung Blues*, the newsletter of the North Carolina chapters of the CBLA. He was the first person in the Carolina Brown Lung Association ever to receive a court-ordered workers' compensation award for brown lung disease. Liberty Mutual Insurance Company, the insurance carrier for J. P. Stevens, had to pay him twenty thousand dollars. The *Brown Lung Blues* carried that news and said that "Otis Edwards used part of his check to install central heating in his house." The dear cost of winter heat—the price of his lungs.

Otis, a thin, dark, noble figure, sat in an armchair waiting for the stew he was making to finish cooking. His gentle-faced wife, Lucy, nimbly worked hook and yarn, crocheting a hat for her sister. Most days the couple sat at home together, Otis disabled since 1973 and Lucy retired from housework since 1971. Both were sixty-seven years old.

"We've been living in Lincoln Heights for thirty-seven years," Lucy said. "We've been in this present house for twelve. Most of these people who live over here in Lincoln Heights do public work."

Public work?

"Yes. Working in the houses or working in the mills, places like that."

"In other words," Otis interjected, "working for somebody else. Not working for yourself, like farming."

"That's right, working in stores and things like that. Way back yonder all the colored here could do was somebody's housework. They ain't been working colored people in the mills but so long."

"We both grew up in the country," Otis said. "My daddy raised cotton, corn, peanuts, and some tobacco. He didn't have enough for what I'd call a 'two-mule crop,' so he worked his own farm, sharecropped, and rented some land."

"His daddy's mama was a slave," Lucy said. "Rhitta Bridges was her name. She used to tell me about slavery times, and about being thirteen when Lee surrendered. That's the way she told her age. That's all she had to go by. When Lee surrendered, I think that the colored people could get away from slavery. I *think* that's what it meant. I never did hear tell how she left."

Otis spoke up. "John Bridges, her second husband, was in the Civil War way back yonder. He got a check from that. She got it after he died."

"She told me she wanted to get away from being a slave, but she couldn't do it," Lucy said. "The way they had you under slavery, you had to do what they said. She had a hard time. I heard tell what a time she had. The white people where she was a slave used to beat them, used to whip them bad. They were just mean to them because they were black. She never did tell us where it was she was a slave.

"She weren't a great talker. She didn't do much talking." Lucy looked up from her crocheting. "You know how some people don't say more than you ask them? That's how she was." She went back to her hook and yarn.

Otis continued. "She told me that when she had to be out there picking cotton when it was so cold, her hands and feet cracked open and bled. What those slaves would do is catch the white folks that they was working for, catch them gone. They'd pull that cotton from the seed, you know, and pick up rocks from the ground and knock them rocks together over the cotton and get a flame going. They'd warm their hands by it."

Otis shook his head over the memory of cotton fields of yore. I thought of the burning tires warming black hands and feet outside in the now.

Otis returned to the story of his own youth. "When I was about ten or twelve years old, my father started hiring me out. He hired me out to Willie Shell, a white man. I'd go there with a plow.

"I'd been behind a mule every day from sun to sun from the time I was seven. My daddy had two mules. The one I worked was called 'Ida.' I'd plow me a clod of dirt. I'd rip me a hard clod of dirt, great big clumps of dirt, you know. They'd knock you in the calf of your leg, and you'd jump. This was when I was seven.

"I worked out in the fields up until I was about seventeen, and I got me this job at the mill rolling coal for the boiler room. That was in 1928. My oldest brother, Jake, was already working over there, and he heard about the job. At that time, the Simmons Company owned the mills. Called it the Rosemary Manufacturing Company. That's where I first started.

"Some blacks always rolled coal and fired up the furnace. That's the only jobs they'd let you do back then, except maybe scrub the bathroom, scrub the floors.

"The train brought in cars of coal. They unloaded them out there into the chute. My job was to roll that wheelbarrow, fill it with coal, and push it into the boiler room for the fire.

"It was pretty dusty out there, but I'd try to stay on the other side when the wind was blowing that coal dust thisaway. You know, when I had my hearing up at the court to get my brown lung compensation, the wife of one of the Industrial Commissioners was there. When she heard about my work at the mill, she said to her husband that she thought I probably had *both* black lung and brown lung.

"I was working ten hours a day then, fifty-five hours a week. I might bring home pay of fourteen dollars."

"It was $14.85," said Lucy, not looking up from her crocheting.

"After I did that for a year or two, they changed the boiler and started using oil. So they transferred me to the dye house. I started out loading the dye kiln. There were two kilns. Each one was about as big as this living room. They're built down into the floor. Me and Lucy's brother, James Ollie Harrison, used to work together. One of us would load, and the other would pack. Then we'd switch over.

"You dye a thousand pounds of cotton at a time. What you do is weigh the first bale and throw it in. Pack it down in that kiln with your feet. The second bale you've got to be more careful with. You'd weigh it. Most bales are five hundred pounds, but some are a little over. You keep taking off sheets of cotton until the bale weighs exactly five hundred pounds. Then you throw that one in the kiln too. You see, the formula for dyeing is set for a thousand pounds exactly.

"Then what you do to make that dye set in the fabric is take two hundred pounds of salt and put it in with the dye and the water. The kiln has a great big heavy lid. If it falled on you, it would kill you. What you do is clamp it down tight all the way. Then throw the lever. Hot water comes pouring down through the top. When it's finished, you throw the other lever, and the water drains out. You'd clean the kiln with cold water. Sometimes you'd change the color two or three times a day.

"Later on, I done the dyeing myself. That was a big promotion. I got about a nickel extra for it. I made the mixtures myself. Like you take green. You've got to mix blue and yellow and get it just right. I liked green best, it was so easy. You take colors like tan and rust. Rust is some kind of hard. You have to get your color mixtures and your temperatures and everything just right."

"That dye got in his clothes and in his skin, and it wouldn't come out," Lucy said. "He ruined all my sheets and towels and all my babies' clothes. He'd come home and pick up the baby. Just by hugging it, he'd get the clothes stained so bad. I was glad when he stopped working up there."

"They laid me off when they closed the dye house. See, they don't dye like that any more. They do the dyeing on the beam, right on the loom. From the dye house I went to the Patterson Mill, stripping cards. When I first went in there, we used to strip the cards every two and a half hours.

"Cards is what you call the machines that knocks all the dirt and lint out of the cotton. They have a big, wide, spongy cylinder. The lint and trash stick to it. To strip, you put a roller in exactly the opposite way the cylinder turns. All that stuff comes off the cylinder and wraps around this roller. Then you take the roller down and twist off all that cotton trash. You put all that stuff in a burlap bag and carry it over to a conveyer that goes to the waste house. Then they use it again.

"They don't strip like that no more. They done changed twice since I've been there. Now they have this cleaning system that's supposed to suck all this lint and dirt from the cards and carry it to the waste house direct.

"I was on that stripping job for thirty years. That's where I got around all that cotton dust. You know, back when I worked there, nobody knowed nothing about no brown lung. I knew there was something wrong because I just started having trouble breathing twenty years before I retired, but I didn't have no idea what it was.

"I retired on January 9, 1973, when I was sixty-two and a half. A couple of years after I left, I joined the Carolina Brown Lung Association and filed my workers' compensation claim. We've been working hard over there, on the cotton-dust standard, on getting people their money from the insurance company, on trying to get the mills to clean up.

"Just before I retired, I was working fifty-two hours a week and bringing home $112. When I left the mill, they gave me two face cloths, two bath towels, a plaque, and $1,100 in profit-sharing.

"Time was, when I was starting out in the mill, I worked in the

yard and brought home pay of only $9.15. Out there raking and so
forth, keeping the lawn clean. That's what they do right now,
have them people—and they're all blacks—out working on the
yard. They get less pay than anybody. I don't know why. I always
thought it was unfair.

"Something they did back then, and it ain't been but forty
years ago, was to have me punch in at the mill and then go over
to my supervisor's house and rake his leaves and cut his grass.
That was old Gerald Cross.

"I remember that first day I worked over at his house. It was
cool. The leaves had fell. They had four or five dogs, and his wife
had set up a little table under an oak tree. A kind of small table
set out with a cup and plate. She said, 'Otis, won't you eat?' I said
to her, 'Thank you very much. I already ate.' See, she wanted me
to sit *outside* under that tree."

"I'm the same way," Lucy said, looking up from her crocheting.
"I don't *never* want to eat if somebody tries to feed me that way."

"They used to treat the blacks any way they wanted. You know
what they did one time back then?" Otis asked. "The master me-
chanic, the boss of the shop, Joe Cox, used to own all them old
houses up around here and where Miz Hattie Baker used to live.
It was hard times back then. He had to do some layoffs.

"I was still living at the old place out in the country then, and
he laid off all of us from out there. See, a lot of them renters he
had out in them houses I was talking about weren't working any-
where. So what he done is lay off us folks who lived in the country
and hired his own folks so he could get his rent." Otis Edwards
shook his head and laughed. Too-quick, rage-covering laughter,
the legacy of a people long and recently oppressed.

Lucy, still crocheting, like a black Madame Defarge knitting
the names of French aristocrats, did not look up. "You don't
know nothing about it," she said with quiet fierceness, "but
colored people weren't more than a dog the way they treated
them."

"That's right," Otis murmured softly; "that's right."

Lucy went on. "Roanoke Rapids used to be a bad town. All
these colored people will tell you that. I got a job over town when
my children got big enough. I first worked for a dollar a day doing

housework. Some of the people were paying fifty cents and some
seventy-five cents. I did cleaning, scrubbing, washing windows,
anything that needed to be done. I'd generally go to work at nine,
but I *always* got back home before sundown.

"I used to work for Archibald Meikle, the superintendent of the
Patterson Mill at that time. I worked in his house, cleaning.
There was a man named Bill Barner who was hired at the mill.
But he did more work around Mr. Meikle's house than he did at
the mill.

"One time two white men were out to get them a nigger. They
spotted Bill Barner and they said, 'There's a nigger. Let's get
him.' Bill Barner was alone and he was coming from church and
he was so scared. The white men got close up to him. One of
them looked at him and said, 'Let's not get him. He's Meikle's
nigger.' That's what saved him."

Otis sat silent. Then another memory surged. "Down at the
mill, they didn't let us drink out of the cooler. We couldn't have
no water unless we brought a glass or a bottle from home to run
the water in. Well, at that time, a black woman who was sweeping over there, Semora Sweat, had brought a glass from home and
laid it alongside the cooler for us blacks to drink out of. That particular morning, an inspector was coming by to see that everything was in order. Before he came, our supervisor, Gerald Cross,
taked it and throwed it in the trash can. I know because I saw him
do it myself.

"After the inspection, Miz Sweat came over to me wanting to
know where her glass was, and I told her. 'Well, how we gonna
drink water?' is what she said. I said, 'I'm gonna drink it just like
they do'; so I started drinking out of the cooler.

"That went on for a couple of days. Then the supervisor sent
his second hand over to tell me the thing about not drinking out
of the cooler. He asked me how I was gonna drink water without
a glass, and I told him, 'I don't care if I drink it just like it is.'

"A day or two after that, this second hand comes back and says
that the supervisor told him, 'If he wants a drink of water, he's
gotta drink out of the bottle.' He said, 'That's what the supervisor
said,' and this second hand walked right on.

"About this same time Frank Williams, Jr., the son of the man who was then running all the mills, was working his way through. He worked on each job in the card room, spinning room, and so forth, one day for each job. They had just promoted him to assistant superintendent. Anyway, he worked with me one day, and he learned me. He learned my name personal, you know.

"So one day, when all this was going on over the water cooler, I run into him as I was going out the stairs, going to the bathroom. See, we was upstairs on the second floor, but when the blacks was ready to go to the bathroom—rain, snow, or shine—we had to go downstairs to the bathroom outside.

"So anyway, I met Mr. Frank Williams, Jr., on the stairs as I was going outside to the bathroom. He said, 'Otis, how are you doing?' I told him, 'I'm doing all right, Mr. Williams, thank you.' But then I said, 'Mr. Williams, I want to tell you what I'm doing.' And I did. I told Mr. Frank Williams, Jr., about drinking out of the cooler. He said, 'Otis, I didn't know about that. I'll have it fixed up right now.'

"He turned around and went back to the shop, and it weren't but thirty minutes before he put up a rack to hold some paper cups. Right then. The same day. He came to me and said, 'Otis, now, when these cups are used up, you don't have to have no order. You go right to the supply room and tell them you want a box of cups.'

"So we broke that up right there." He paused a moment, then added, "You know right *then* I felt like it was a nice thing for him to do. But I *still* feel like we should drink the same like they do."

Otis got up to go to the kitchen and check on his stew.

"Is he a good cook?" I asked.

"He can cook easy things," Lucy said. "He does pretty good."

"My wife eats it," Otis called from the kitchen.

"I'd rather eat his cooking than a lot of others," Lucy said.

"You know," she went on, "I used to work some for Mr. Frank Williams, the big boss. I used to go down and help iron and clean. I weren't there by the day. I'd just go once a week and iron. When I finished that, I'd help that colored lady who worked there clean, you know, to make my day out. I did that, I guess, about a year and a half.

"His son, Frank Williams, Jr., wasn't living there then, but he came by once, and he was just as nice as he could be. Mrs. Williams too. She was a nice lady. But the old man weren't. He was just as *rebish* as he could be."

Rebish?

"You know, *rebish*—hateful to black people. He wouldn't speak to you. He'd walk on your toes. I don't mean on top of them; I mean he'd walk over you and not speak to you."

Otis had come back into the room. He remembered something else. "When J. P. Stephenson come here, he gave us a Christmas dinner. They had barbecue, Brunswick stew, anything you could want. Only thing was, all the blacks had to take their meal out there in the warehouse where there was no heat. All the whites were inside the mill in the cloth room, where it was clean and warm. Then that law got passed. That civil rights law.

"Shearod Crumpler was the superintendent up at the mill then. He was a *rebish* soul too. He didn't like blacks. But he came out there, closed the department down, got us all in a group, and told us that the law had passed. He said, 'Any of the blacks that's qualified to run these jobs, any jobs, we're going to let them have it.' Then he talked about the bathroom. He said, 'The blacks don't have to go down the stairs and outside no more. They can use the same bathroom.' Then he got through talking.

"Well, I was the only black male working on daytime shift. After Crumpler got through talking, my own supervisor come over to me and said, 'Otis,' he said, 'when you go in the bathroom and you got to use the commode, use the first one.'" Otis laughed. "I didn't pay him no mind. Because we'd heard about the law, read about it; it was on television. So I used whatever one I wanted to.

"After that, things turned around *some*. That first Christmas after the civil rights law, J. P. Stephenson had us all together for dinner. Well, actually, there weren't but two blacks on first shift —me and Arlene Hines. She was a sweeper.

"Anyway, this white man came up to me and Arlene. He had one of those old toys making fun of black people. One of those doll babies with red lips and everything. Well, just as we were all praying over our food, he set that thing to dancing real close to Arlene and me. As soon as the blessing was over, I got up, taking my plate with me, and Arlene did too. We went down to the other end of the table and sat there."

Otis was not laughing. He looked directly at me. "You can't go to heaven when you don't treat people right. I reckon a lot of them is in hell for the way they treated colored people."

For My Black Brothers
and Sisters

LUCY SLEDGE

Lucy Edwards' niece and namesake, Lucy Sledge, lived in Hodges-town, the black community within the Roanoke Rapids city limits. The Sledges lived on Queen Street, a deeply rutted, dirt road, with lofty-named neighbors—Duke, Prince, and King streets. The only nobility is in the spirit of its inhabitants like Lucy Sledge. Like her Uncle Otis, Lucy Sledge contributed a historic precedent for southern textile workers fighting for justice. She brought the initial race discrimination suit against J. P. Stevens and Company.

Lucy was thirty, striking and stylish. She wore hoop earrings, neatly pressed khakis, and a T-shirt. Her ten-year-old, Stephanie, was in school. Her younger daughter, Melody, and Melody's cousin Tammy were both home for the day recovering from slight colds and basking in Lucy's mother-coddling. The two children, both dressed in long flowered flannel nightgowns, sat in a thick band of sunlight by the trailer's kitchen window, spooning vegetable soup.

Lucy took a chair where she could watch the children and talked about her experiences.

For twelve years she had gone to the John Armstrong Chaloner School in Hodgestown, Roanoke Rapids' only black school. "When I was at school, there was no integration at all. And at that time, they gave us the books that the whites had finished with three years before.

"A couple of years ago, after integration, the whites took over the Chaloner School. Now the school board is putting $300,000 into improvements for the school. They didn't do that when it was black.

"Now that burns me up: blacks paying city taxes and having to send their own children out into the county to school. The way the Roanoke Rapids school board has everything worked out, the city schools are almost all white. They do what they want to. As long as the whites can keep us down, they'll keep on doing us like they are."

Lucy Sledge talked about her adolescence. "When we were growing up, all we were allowed to watch on television was the news. Everything that was going on then stayed on my daddy's mind. It was all his talk. It was always what was happening somewhere else—Selma, Birmingham, Montgomery—not here. So my sisters and me just wanted to do something here.

"In 1965, when I was seventeen and still in high school, me and three or four of my sisters were sitting in the car in front of Hudson's Grill over on the Avenue, near the *Daily Herald* office, not far from where the union hall is now. We were just sitting there. You know how teen-agers are. We kept saying to one another, 'You go in first.' 'No, *you* go first!' We were scared because we knew they were so hateful.

"Still we wanted to go in. We wanted to do *something*. They were so *rebish*, so prejudiced. We just wanted to get served some food. When we finally got the courage to go in, the man behind the counter took a pistol out. We left in a hurry.

"My sisters brought that man to court, but nothing happened. He said it was a stick and not a gun. My sisters said they knew the difference between a stick and a gun.

"Hudson's got forced out of town after that. They were so hateful. The NAACP told them if they didn't integrate, they'd padlock the door. They're operating out in the county under a different name, and it's integrated now. I know because my husband goes in there to eat, but I won't.

"My father was proud of me and my sisters. He thought we did right. Later, when I went into court against J. P. Stevens, he called me up and told me again that he was proud of me. He told me, 'You're the only black to stand up for blacks. You've done right.'

"There has been a lot of hate here," Lucy said. "The year after that, in 1966, they had a big KKK rally right in that field outside, just where you turn into Queen Street. Can you imagine that? Holding a thing like that *here* where it's all black. They had big signs on the road advertising it and everything."

A week before the rally was held, members of the Halifax and Northampton branches of the NAACP, the Halifax County Voters Movement, and the Student Nonviolent Coordinating Committee (SNCC) filed a petition to city, county, state, and federal officials protesting the "rally in an all-Negro neighborhood." Their objections went unheeded.

Two and a half hours before the rally was scheduled to begin, a local black man, shooting from a car, fired eight shots from a semiautomatic .22-caliber rifle. Two white men were wounded, including a Klan security guard. A bullet passed through the shirt of another man, who was helping erect the speakers' platform. None was injured seriously enough to keep him from the rally.

By the time the rally began, between 150 and 200 police officers had gathered to protect the assembled whites. All available highway patrol cars were on the scene, as well as officers and men from the Roanoke Rapids police, the sheriffs' departments of Halifax and Northampton counties and the State Bureau of Investigation.

As the rally started, ten blacks, six of them juveniles, began picketing. They were promptly arrested and charged with walking on the wrong side of the highway. Then about twenty-five more pickets were arrested as they converged on the field. Police reported that the arrests were made to avert "an outburst of violence."

"My husband, David, was one of those arrested. He was passing out leaflets at the time. Well, they had their meeting," Lucy conceded grimly, "but I'll tell you one thing: After that, they didn't stage another rally in Hodgestown.

"That was the year I graduated from high school and started working at Stevens. I was a single-needle operator hemming terry cloth towels at the Fabricating Plant, and I made $1.25 an hour."

An afternoon in Halifax, the county seat.

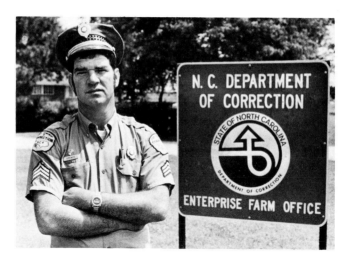

The old Tillery plantation, now the largest farm in Halifax County.

The politicians.

Former cotton pickers displaced by agricultural mechanization.

In August 1967 Lucy was transferred to "banding and binding" in the same plant.

"You know, there are some things you don't need anyone to tell you," Lucy said. "You can see for yourself. Like back when I started with Stevens, they weren't hiring any 'ugly blacks.' I hate to say that, but I don't know another way to put it. All I know is there were no 'ugly blacks' in there. You had to be light and nice-looking. Now, I can't call myself beautiful, but I am light-skinned.

"I worked up there until November 1967. Then I left J. P. Stevens on maternity leave to have my first child. She was born in February 1968.

"Right after the baby was born, Stevens fired my husband, David, for holding down two jobs. He was working for the A&P, and it's union. If they even *thought* you were for the union, they'd fire you. His bossman asked him, since David was working for the A&P, wasn't he for the union? It wasn't two nights after that that David was fired.

"I personally had no experience with unions. I do remember seeing a black girl wearing a union pin back in 1967 or 1968, and they fired her. Back then, if you were for the union, you were real quiet about it. I had already been laid off before they won the election here.

"Anyway," Lucy continued, "I went back to Stevens in April 1968. I was working as a terry inspector. I worked until July, when they laid off two of us—me and a white girl. They told us no work was available. Not long after that, I saw that white girl that got laid off with me over town. She said, 'I have my job back. You should go over to the personnel office.' I went back to the personnel office seven times, and they said they had nothing."

When Lucy was laid off, her supervisor filled out a termination form. It said that the quality and quantity of her work, her conduct and attendance, and her attitude toward other employees were all good. He recommended that Lucy Sledge be re-employed, and he wrote that he wanted her to return to his department in the future.

Then Stevens hired several white women who had work experience inferior to hers and less education. And the company rehired a number of people it had previously fired, former employees whose supervisors had recommended against re-employing them, former employees with poor attendance records and poor work records. They even rehired one white woman who had quit or been discharged fourteen times. During the last seven months of 1969 they hired four white women and no blacks for terry inspector jobs. But J. P. Stevens did not rehire or recall Lucy Sledge.

"Always when you went into the Stevens personnel office," Lucy said, "it was mostly blacks waiting, on the porch, inside, everywhere. We'd sit there. Every time a white comes out of that office, they'd have an envelope. Now I know what that means because I already worked there; it means you have the job. It's the papers to carry you to the doctor for a physical examination. But when we'd ask the whites when they came out of the office, 'Did you get a job?' they'd say they didn't.

"Sometimes you'd sit there all day. I remember old man Dickens. He's a white man. One time, when it was my turn to go into his office, he shouted at me, 'Don't sit down! And don't you call on me no more unless I call on you.'

"Now, I didn't have a telephone at that time, so there was no way he could call me. And I knew he wasn't going to write me a letter.

"When my husband came home, I told him what happened at the personnel office. I said, 'David, they shouldn't be doing that. Much as I need a job, there were some in there that looked like they needed one even worse. They shouldn't be doing what they're doing.' He told me, 'There's nothing that can be done.'

"I just wanted to do *something*. So I called Reginald Harrison. He's my first cousin. His father was James Ollie, my mother's brother, who used to work up there at the mill with Uncle Otis. I told Reginald what happened, and he put me in touch with the Equal Employment Opportunity Commission. Then in March 1970 I filled out a discrimination complaint.

"I didn't hear from the EEOC for about thirty days. Then they sent some people up from Atlanta. Finally they gave me a notice that I had thirty more days in which I had the right to sue. And they told me they were proud of me.

"Then I got a lawyer, Richard Seymour." Seymour is a Washington-based attorney, now working for the Lawyers' Committee for Civil Rights Under Law. "It took a long time after that. The lawyer was getting everything ready and making sure everything I said was true. I went to court in Raleigh for five days." *Sledge* v. *J. P. Stevens and Company* was a class-action discrimination suit on behalf of all blacks employed at the J. P. Stevens plants in Roanoke Rapids. "I was scared, scared to go. I was afraid something was going to happen to me.

"On the second or third day of the trial, J. P. Stevens brought in about thirty blacks. They were all dressed up and everything, and they just sat there. I was on one side of the courtroom. J. P. Stevens had all those other blacks sitting there on the other side against me. And there I was trying to help them.

"Believe it or not, my Uncle Otis was there. When I saw him, I said, 'Uncle Otis, what are you doing here?' He said, 'I don't know. They just told me to come.' He looked kind of surprised to see me.

"Now I could expect this of Stevens, that they would try to do something like this. But I couldn't understand those blacks being there. Stevens couldn't get me there without my knowing what I was there for. Those blacks were being used and didn't know it. They probably got the day off with pay.

"Stevens had their big officials in court testifying against me." A. Edwin Akers, Stevens' administrative assistant in Roanoke Rapids, who had also been employed by the Simmons Company, took the witness stand, as he would also do in defense of Stevens' labor policies.

Richard Seymour questioned Akers on the mill company's role in fostering inequality between black and white employees. Akers had offered as one explanation for the advancement of whites over blacks in the mills the fact that the whites had had superior industrial training. He testified that in the 1930s and early 1940s the Simmons Company had lent, free of charge, a loom and other textile equipment to the all-white Roanoke Rapids high school's textile department.

"This is interesting information about the school system," U. S. District Court Judge Franklin T. Dupree, Jr., said. Then the Court addressed Akers directly. "Were any of these educational facilities available to blacks?"

"No, sir," Akers answered.

"What about the black schools, did they have comparable facilities?"

"No, they did not have comparable facilities."

Judge Dupree questioned Akers further. "You say then they
were not only separate but unequal."

"Yes, they were," Akers replied.

Under cross-examination Akers said that the mill company had
not seen fit to lend textile equipment to Roanoke Rapids' black
school. He added that the black school had not asked for it. Had
the white school asked for the equipment, the plaintiff's attorney
asked? Akers answered that he thought the school board had
approved the request.

One of the charges in the *Sledge* v. *J. P. Stevens* case was that
at Stevens' Roanoke Rapids plants a black person with a twelfth-
grade education was treated like a white person with a fourth-
grade education. J. P. Stevens offered no evidence to explain the
disparate treatment given to Lucy Sledge, but it did address the
class-action charge of discrimination.

Defense attorney Whiteford Blakeney, who represented Stevens
in many labor law suits, summarized the company's defense: "Let
me take the analogy of the race. This track I'm talking about is
straight, and it tends to go uphill. It's inclined because uphill is
where the better jobs are and the high pay is. Now, at the beginning of this track, who came to the track first? Mr. Akers made
that very clear: White people got started on the track first. Is
that because the company wouldn't let the Negroes on the track?

"Now, your Honor, let's follow Mr. Akers' analogy. He presented it, I thought, so clearly. Mr. Akers said the track was there,
that Negroes were not barred from it; they didn't come to it
much to start with.

"I repeat," Blakeney continued, "the company wasn't saying to
the Negro, 'It's no use for you to try, you can't have it.' They
weren't saying that to him. But the Negro said to himself, 'I can't
win the job, and I know I can't.' And so they didn't try; except
some. And of those, some did all right.

"Now then, the whites started on the run and therefore they
got the jobs at that point. Many of them are still there and naturally they're ahead. They started sooner. Because the Negro didn't
choose to start with them.

"Now today, the whites have quit coming there to get into that race as they once did. Why? They've gone on to higher-paying industries. That's why. The Negro is better able to compete today and he realizes that and he comes in greater and greater volume."

In his December 1975 finding, Judge Dupree said that because J. P. Stevens hired substantial numbers of blacks during the period in question and because no evidence had been produced of Lucy Sledge's dates of applications or of vacancies on those dates, "the Court cannot assume that this plaintiff was singled out for rejection simply because she was black. Her personal action therefore must fail."

However, addressing himself to the class-action charge of discrimination in J. P. Stevens' Roanoke Rapids plants, Dupree ruled: "The Court therefore concludes that Stevens has *purposefully* discriminated against blacks on the basis of their race in hiring, initial assignment to job categories and to departments, present job assignments, promotions, transfers between departments, layoffs and recalls, in imposing disproportionally long waiting periods upon black female applicants and in reserving certain job categories for whites and others for blacks."

J. P. Stevens appealed Dupree's decision on the finding of discrimination, and Lucy Sledge's attorney appealed the finding on her personal claim. On October 4, 1978, the U. S. Court of Appeals for the Fourth Circuit upheld Dupree's finding of discrimination at Stevens' Roanoke Rapids plants and reversed his decision on Lucy Sledge, giving her the opportunity to pursue her claim in court.

As she watched the children in her trailer on Queen Street, Lucy Sledge said, "I did do right. I know I did. I'd go down for this, if I had to, for my black brothers and sisters."

Memorabilia

A. EDWIN AKERS

At home, in his paneled den, A. Edwin Akers drew a rough map of Roanoke Rapids' school district. "You know, you can live within city limits and not be in the city school district, and you can live within the school district and not be in the city," Akers said as he sketched in the John Armstrong Chaloner School in Hodgestown, at the very edge of the city school district.

In the old days the John Armstrong Chaloner School had been the only black grade and high school in Roanoke Rapids. The man who built the first mill in town had donated ten acres of land in 1924 for the express purpose of building a school for blacks.

The J. P. Stevens executive was explaining how the Roanoke Rapids school board dealt with federally enforced integration. "I was on the school board at the time, and we found that there was no land beyond the Chaloner School in the Roanoke Rapids school district. We could simply draw a line around the Chaloner School and eliminate it from the school district without affecting the population."

To demonstrate, Akers took the pen again and drew a thick line around the black school, isolating it. "And that's what we did.

"At the time, the John Armstrong Chaloner School had about eleven hundred students. Eight hundred of them were from out in the county. When it came time to integrate, some of us on the school board went up to Washington to present our integration plan. We told them, 'We can integrate inside our district, we can take care of our own three hundred, but we have eight hundred students coming from out in the county.' And they said to us, 'Well, give them back to the county.' Of course, you couldn't do this overnight," Akers said. "They didn't have the facilities in the county.

"So what we on the school board did"—he pointed again to his hand-drawn map with the black school excluded from the city school district—"was to let the county use the Chaloner School for four years to give it time to build its own schools. Then in 1971 the city's school district border was changed back again, and the Chaloner School was reopened as a middle school."

After the Chaloner School was reopened as a city school in 1971, it was predominantly white. When Lucy Sledge attended the school in the 1960s, it had been completely black.

"Chaloner used to give presents to each boy and girl in school in Roanoke Rapids," Akers said. "I know an older woman who still has the doll that John Armstrong Chaloner gave her when she was a schoolchild."

He put aside the map and took down from the bookshelf behind him a purple book with gold and red lettering. It was a copy of *Robbery Under Law*. Inside, the inscription read: "School Superintendent Akers, compliments of the author, John Armstrong Chaloner, 'The Merry Mills.'"

"You know that my father was the first superintendent of schools in Roanoke Rapids," Akers said. Alonzo Edwin Akers, Edwin's father, was a sixth-generation Virginian, a descendent of slave owners, who grew up in the valley of the Blackwater River, in his great-grandfather Samuel Akers' house. Alonzo attended a log-hewn schoolhouse outfitted with straight benches and a cast-iron stove. He learned from Webster's Blue-Back Speller and McGuffey's Readers.

When he was eighteen, Alonzo Akers began teaching in a one-room Virginia schoolhouse for seventeen dollars and fifty cents a month. His mother had always made his clothing, weaving the cloth on her hand loom. Alonzo grew popcorn commercially to buy his first suit. Then he borrowed fifteen dollars from his father's cousin to pay his way to Piedmont Normal School in Rocky Mount, Virginia. Next he traveled to North Carolina to teach school in Henderson, fifty miles from Roanoke Rapids. In 1908 he

was hired by the Roanoke Rapids school district as the first superintendent of schools.

For the first eleven years the mill town did not have its own
school. In 1907 the Roanoke Rapids Graded School District was
chartered. The next year Roanoke Rapids built two schools and
initiated compulsory four-month school attendance. That first
year 183 pupils studied under the direction of Alonzo Akers.

"Now in those days," Edwin Akers said, "the mill owners were
a little bit paternalistic. They built medical clinics, canneries, and
recreation centers. They established a medical system, and they
were very active in planning the school system. The facilities we
had then were quite advanced for a little town.

"The reason the schools in Roanoke Rapids were outstanding
was because some of the early leaders of Roanoke Rapids, and particularly people like Mr. Sam Patterson, were very forward-look-
ing, very progressive people. And the townspeople have always
supported the schools."

John Patterson sat on Roanoke Rapids' first school board. Later
his brother Sam served on the board. The mills made large dona-
tions to the schools and, during one financially difficult period, actually financed the day-to-day operations.

And the mills got what they needed. Under Alonzo Akers, business education classes and industrial arts were introduced into the
curriculum in 1912. Throughout the 1930s the Roanoke Rapids
high school's textile department used the loom that Edwin Akers
had testified about in the *Sledge* v. *J. P. Stevens* case. In 1939 a
gift of land was instrumental in getting an adequate building for a
new textile school.

"To get the flavor of those early days, take a look at this 1918
"Progress" edition of the *Daily Herald*," Edwin Akers said, pointing to a front-page story.

The article said, "The 'atmosphere' in Roanoke Rapids is first
of all energetic. The town is not hampered by useless precedent or
tradition in its community progress. Not one of its adult citizens
was born here, but most of them have witnessed the larger part
of its development and many have developed themselves with the
development of the town. There are no idle rich, no leisure class.
The shirker, the slacker, the loafer, find little here congenial."

Another page-one article was written by Akers' father, who had become the school superintendent for Halifax County in 1915. Alonzo Akers said that Halifax County had the largest black school population in North Carolina and that the county's white school population ranked seventeenth in the state. "This means," Alonzo Akers wrote, "that white children are widely scattered and hard to get into large schools."

Like a good teacher, Edwin Akers used a number of visual aids to explain what he was saying. He took a slim bound volume entitled *The Spirit of the Roanoke: A Pageant of Halifax County History* from the shelf behind him. "This was an outdoor drama put on by the county schools. I was there, but because I was in school in town, I had no part in it." Inside, the book said that the play had been "designed and written in collaboration by Halifax County Teachers under the direction of A. E. Akers, County Superintendent."

Edwin Akers thumbed through the book. In a scene set outside the courthouse in Halifax in 1776 one speaker says, "Heaps of things has happened here. . . . It's jest lak I been a-tellin' you. Us in Halifax is gwine to paddle our own canoe and this whole North Carolina is too."

Later on "two negro mammies bring in the spinning wheels and stools for a group of girls" who enter and begin to work and sing, "Oh, yes, I am a Southern Girl, And glory in the name."

At the climax of the pageant "the Spirit of the Roanoke is seated on the central throne, with the New Day at her right hand. The throne on her left remains vacant for Progress." The figure of Industry speaks:

> "I am Industry. . . .
> The endless whir of intricate machinery is mine,
> And power of steam, electricity and steel.
> From you, oh mighty Roanoke, long has come
> A rich supply of power to turn my wheels.
> How I shall be developed, best guided and controlled,
> Looms now a mammoth problem on before you."

Then Edwin Akers turned to the personal. He took out a photograph of his mother, Ivy Virginia Pridgen, standing by the River Mill dressed in a long white dress and broad black hat. "My mother came here in 1909 to teach for my father, but when she married, she couldn't teach. There's no doubt about it, we discriminated against women then."

Akers had a photograph of his father too, dressed in suit and tie, standing by the bulkhead built by Major Thomas Emry when he was first harnessing the power of the Roanoke River. A third photograph was of the substantial house on Roanoke Avenue where the five Akers children grew up. "People used to say, 'Did you know there is a house in Roanoke Rapids that covers seven Akers?' Edwin said with a smile.

The Akers house was one block from the old Alonzo E. Akers School, which Frankie Wood had reluctantly attended, and one block from the New Mill. Behind the house was the Stevens administration building.

Alonzo and Ivy Virginia's children were pulled more toward the mill than toward the school. Edwin's brother Henry worked as a cost manager at the Stevens offices behind his childhood home. His sister Lois was the widow of Shearod Crumpler, who had been the superintendent of the Patterson Mill when Otis Edwards worked there. Edwin himself was the highest local-born official at J. P. Stevens' Roanoke Rapids plants.

"I started out to be a teacher," Edwin said. "I got my B.A. in Education at the University of North Carolina, but I wasn't meant for teaching. Also, in 1934, salaries for teachers were only seventy dollars a month, eight months a year. And my ability was in administration, so I ended up by working forty-three years in the textile mills here."

With the drawing of the gerrymandered Roanoke Rapids school district at his feet and the memorabilia of education in the mill town surrounding him, Edwin Akers added, "I've tried to make some contribution to the schools here by being on the school board."

Sons of the Soil

JAMES BOONE AND LEWIS EDWARDS

In addition to racism in Roanoke Rapids schools, racism in the mills was overt. In the early days of the mills, long before the Civil Rights Act of 1964 and the subsequent influx of blacks into the textile industry, the mills had tried to keep white employees in line by threatening to replace them with blacks.

After federally enforced integration changed the racial makeup of the textile work force, mills updated their methods and tried to fan racism in order to keep black and white workers from joining forces.

Because the workers in many southern mills that voted for union representation were predominantly black, blacks represented the threat of unionization to mill owners. Although 23 per cent of J. P. Stevens' employees were black, in Roanoke Rapids 40 per cent of the Stevens workers were black.

During the 1974 union organizing drive in Roanoke Rapids that resulted in a union victory, J. P. Stevens officials had intimated—in captive-audience speeches—that to join the union was to submit to a black-dominated organization. Stevens employed other, crasser tactics as well. The company posted on its plant bulletin board a photograph of the white victims of the "Zebra killings," the racially inspired murders by black terrorists in San Francisco.

To their credit, large numbers of white mill workers rose above their racist social and industrial milieu. Lewis Edwards was one of these. Unlike many white mill workers, whose families had labored for generations in the textile industry, Lewis Edwards considered himself a farmer first. This tie with the land gave him more in common with rural blacks, newly hired in the mills, than with older, white mill workers with their long experience with the mill's history of paternalism.

At ten-thirty in the evening, Lewis Edwards came in from work, his trousers and boots caked with earth. He had not been home for thirteen hours. That morning he had left his brick house, on a street not far from the New Mill, to work as an electrician in the River Mill. Then, when the first shift got off at four, Lewis drove to the 2½-acre sweet potato farm he rented in the county. After that, he stopped by his father's farm to help out there. He had just driven back to Roanoke Rapids and had a few hours to relax before sleeping and starting his double-shift work again the next day.

Lewis greeted his wife, Shelby, a third-generation Roanoke Rapids mill worker, and the couple's two school-age children, who had been waiting up for their father's return.

Lewis pulled off his boots and settled into a chair. He was thirty-five years old and handsome, with smoothed-down, brown hair, a strong jaw, and a steady gaze. He had been working for J. P. Stevens for nearly fifteen years and on the land almost all his life.

When he was two weeks old, his father moved the family from Brunswick, Virginia, to a hundred-acre farm in Gaston, North Carolina. The Edwardses lived on a rural road between Clarence and Hazel Brooks' small house and the eighteen-dollar-a-month shanty surrounded by corn fields that Ernestine and Clarence Brooks, Jr., rented from a white farmer.

Lewis Edwards' father was the first in the family to work in the mills. "Daddy was always working in the cotton mill and on the farm too. He was a watchman in the River Mill. Then he went into the shop as a pipe fitter. He worked forty hours during the week at the mill and then came home at night and worked the farm. Then, in addition to farming and pipe fitting, he started toting the clock at the mill thirty to forty-two hours on weekends to make extra money.

"Me and my brother started working the farm as soon as we

were old enough. Daddy started paying us two cents a pound for picking cotton when we were around nine or ten years old. Before that we were just playing around and didn't get paid.

"When we were kids, me and my brothers, we just wanted to get to Warren Bridge Creek and go fishing or go swimming or catch a little coon or a rabbit.

"But when we got to working, we'd pick a hundred pounds of cotton all day, and we'd get two dollars. We got twenty-five cents for a shock of peanuts, although years on it got to be fifty cents.

"I remember when we bought the first tractor, a Ford. I was about eleven years old. Before that we worked the hundred acres with two mules. Sometimes we hired colored help too. We'd take the truck down and go over to Gumberry and around. You'd just go up to the houses and ask for help, and the next morning go out again and pick up a truckload."

Lewis remembered, too, a story from his adolescence. He leaned forward, clasped his hands loosely in front of him, and said, "One time, I'd taken my mama's car. I think it was the time I was going on my first date with Shelby. Anyway, I was going down the road past our farm, and there were a group of colored—blacks—standing in the middle of the road, and they wouldn't get out of the way. So I just drove real fast by them, and one of them got knocked in the ditch.

"I went on up the road and found the deputy sheriff in Gaston and told him about it. He told me not to worry about it, to go on ahead to my party. Later he told me he'd gone back down the road and couldn't find nobody there, so I guess nobody got hurt too bad. Well, my mama didn't like me driving her car too much after that."

Lewis's recollection was also the story of how he started working in the mill. "My daddy had always told us, me and my brothers, 'Boys, you find something to do besides working in the cotton mill. I don't want you-all to work in a cotton mill around here.' But when I was seventeen, I wanted a car of my own. So first I drove the school bus and then for about three years, I went to school half a day and worked second shift in the New Mill. Got me a job doffing. I thought I could get me a car and then find something else to do, but I'm still there.

"I remember when the union first came in, I didn't know much about it. But I was for it because I was only making two and a quarter an hour. I just wanted to better my pay. Those guys over at the Albemarle Paper Company, down here across from the River Mill, they're union. And they're making four and five dollars an hour. One of these guys comes over to me and starts making fun of me, you know. 'You're making chicken feed,' he says. That's the way they talk. So, they're for the union, you're for the union.

"Back in '65, when the union first come in, I was scared. Then you couldn't, you know, say to your buddy, 'Hey, vote for the union.' If you did, you was in trouble. He's liable to go back and tell the Man you're for the union. If he did, you were gone. You were fired. So if you were for the union, you kept your mouth shut.

"The union lost that 1965 election, but then in 1974 when we won, you were free to come out, more or less. But a lot of them over there are still scared."

Some of the early union meetings in Roanoke Rapids were held in black churches in the county, and Lewis went. "Well, very few whites wanted to go out there, but, you know, it's as hard for them to come into Roanoke Rapids as it was for the whites to go out there. It wasn't easy at first, but we stuck together, blacks and whites, and now we've got our union."

The next day I met another son of the soil, a twenty-seven-year-old black Stevens worker named James Boone. He was a stockman and checker in the Delta Number Four Plant. He worked in the warehouse and was paid two rates: $3.14 for packing and $3.40 for checking. Most days, when he got off work, Boone stopped by the union hall to see what needed to be done. This day it was a mailing, and he operated an antiquated Addressograph as we talked.

He had grown up in the small town of Gumberry, ten miles from Roanoke Rapids. "There ain't no work over there, just farms." It was where, I remembered, Lewis Edwards had gone with his father to pick up extra farm help. James also helped his father. Haywood Boone had been a sharecropper, and James remembered being out with his whole family picking cotton on a white man's farm the day that President Kennedy was shot.

James Boone and Lewis Edwards both spent their childhoods picking cotton, shucking beans, shaking peanuts. Like Lewis, James earned money driving the school bus, each in his segregated school.

Now the two were brought together by the union. Both sat on the ACTWU negotiation committee and fought the same fight, nurtured by the same dreams.

I asked James when he first saw the mills—a question that had made Louis Harrell laugh, since there had never been a time when the mill wasn't central in his life.

"Now the first time I ever saw Roanoke Rapids was going for a ride with some friends from high school. Just riding, you know, just to look. I remember I saw the Patterson plant when I came to town. I wondered why they had barbed-wire fence around it. I didn't know if it was to keep the people in or out.

"Then I heard an ad on the radio for jobs at Stephenson. The chief of police in Seaboard, not far from Gumberry, helped me get my job. He wrote a reference for me. I worked as a doffer in Patterson the latter part of 1970 and part of 1971.

"I couldn't stay with the job. It was hard, and I just quit. I went to Washington, D.C., and worked in a shoe store for six months. Then I came back home and got married and went back to Stephenson.

"I remember in 1974, that first day I seen the union come in here, someone was outside the plant passing out leaflets with little blue cards on them. I took one of those union cards, filled it out, and sent it off. Even before the first meeting we went up to the motel to talk to the organizers. We were rarin' to go."

Why, if he'd just heard of unions, was he so quick to join?

"I felt like it couldn't be bad. I guess it was being black. I was already treated bad.

"Now I leaflet every chance I get. It's funny. People call you crazy standing out there. They do. Or they say, 'You-all tired standing out here?' They won't look at you when you hand them the leaflets. People will be cussin' you out before they get to you. It makes it hard because, you know, if people refuse to even take a leaflet— I would have took it and read it. I wouldn't have been *dumb* to the fact.

"Blacks, I believe, and some whites too, are gonna make some changes here. That's why I come here to the union hall and work so hard. That's why I get out there and leaflet in the cold, in the raw, and in the heat of summer.

"This company's hard to deal with. People here know that. They know about Statesboro, Georgia, too, and how the company shut down the plant there after the union got in. They know about that. And they know that a boycott, which is what the union is doing, means a strong, long-term commitment from us. Because they know a successful boycott means a cutback in orders and that means a slowdown of work. So we have to be committed.

"People know it would be suicide to have a strike here. They know that. J.P. owns eighty-three plants. They could easily ship the work from here to other plants. People know how uphill this battle is. What we are doing here at the union is working to make a better living, decent wages and better benefits. That's what we're fighting for."

Remembering the fear, embedded or overcome, in some of the older, white mill workers, I asked James if he was scared. He looked at me quizzically.

"Scared? Scared of what? There ain't but two things Stephenson can do: They can send me back home or either fire me. I've already told my wife, 'If they fire me, you're going to have to go back home to your mama and daddy, and I'm going to have to go back home to mine until I get a job.' If Stephenson blackballs you, you can't get a job within forty miles."

James laughed. "It tickles me when you say 'scared.' It really tickles me. You know, I'm wondering the way you say that, scared of what? The only one thing I'm scared of is the devil, that he's gonna get me. You know I believe I can get up and go. But I think it's *sad* when a person believes in something and won't stand and fight for it."

I took the thirteen-mile, generations-long road out into the country to visit Dorothy and Haywood Boone. A road like the one traveled many decades before by the Harrells, and then by the Woods, and more recently by Lewis Edwards. A road much longer for the Boones, who were black and had to walk in the gutter and only before sundown.

I drove away from Roanoke Rapids, through the fields of peanuts, corn, and cotton that start on the outskirts of town, away from the white industrial enclave into agricultural, mostly black Northampton County.

In Gumberry, where James Boone was born, the rusted cotton gin stood idle. Farther out, I drove between cotton fields where men and women had labored since long before Major Emry thought to harness the water power of the Roanoke River, long before John Armstrong Chaloner built the first mill that changed this southern landscape.

Past a ramshackle sewing factory, where Lucy Sledge had sewn ladies' garments after she was laid off by J. P. Stevens, past Seaboard's two gas stations and one grocery store, I pulled off the hard-top and onto a dirt road. The Boones lived in the second green house.

A plump woman with an orange and blue bandanna was rocking on the porch. Dorothy Boone was wearing a cotton print dress and red slippers. Haywood Boone, in a John Deere cap, came from the garden behind the house.

I introduced myself, and, after a moment of confusion when I mentioned James—to them their son James Melvin is plain Melvin—we settled down on the porch. I talked to Haywood first so he could get back to his garden. His answers were as spare as his build.

"I worked on a white man's farm. His name was Stephenson. I was half-sharing. Like on a bale of cotton, he gets one half and I get the other. About three or four other colored fellows worked for Stephenson just like I did. He raised cotton, corn, and soybeans. We worked from seven in the morning until six at night. Two of us fellows plowed. It was a two-horse crop. I took care of the horse too.

"You know a lot of people around here are named Stephenson. The Stephenson I worked for, his daddy was the high sheriff in Jackson. I don't think he's no relation to the Stephenson that has the mill over in Roanoke Rapids. The Stephenson I worked for was nice people."

Haywood Boone looked over at me taking notes and added, "I never asked him for nothing but he didn't give it to me. Stephen-

son was real good." Then Haywood Boone chuckled. "I'm giving
him a good name.

"Then I left Stephenson's farm, and I started with Georgia-
Pacific's paper mill. When I first went down there, I was making
$1.95 an hour cleaning up outside the mill. They had a strike over
there, they did. After that I got to go inside, patching boards,
and I've been inside ever since. Now I make $3.76 an hour.

"See, they had a small union come in there, they did. That was
the first I heard about a union. I joined it that day. The other
fellows asked me if I was gonna join. I said yeah, if they joined, I
was gonna join it too. I didn't want to be odd from the rest of
them." Haywood proudly produced his International Woodcut-
ters Union of America membership card, then carefully replaced
it in his wallet.

What did Haywood know about J. P. Stevens?

"I didn't know a thing about the cotton mills in Roanoke
Rapids until my boy went over there to work at it. See, back a
time, the colored folk couldn't even go into Roanoke Rapids."

Dorothy Boone, who had been rocking and listening, addressed
no one in particular: "They didn't like colored folks."

"Now you can mix and get along with white people a whole lot
lovelier together than used to be," Haywood added.

Had Haywood told his son about the racial situation in the mill
town?

"No. He didn't know nothin' about no Roanoke Rapids. What
he knows, he just knows by hearing and doing."

How did he feel about his son working in the mill in a white
town? Even today Roanoke Rapids is 87 per cent white in a
county that is 51 per cent black.

"I feel all right about it. I didn't want none of my children to
farm. But every day and every night I told him not to give them
no trouble."

After her husband went back to the garden, Dorothy Boone
and I stayed on the porch. Then she began her story, which she
told in rhythms in unison with her rocking.

"I never done nothing." Rock forward. "But work on the
farm." Rock back. "First with my father." Rock. "Then with my
husband. We worked on the farm. Like work by the day. Shuckin'
beans. Till I was grown.

"We had to walk." Rock. "Two or three miles." Rock. "To school. I went to the fourth grade." Rock. "Then I got grown." Rock. "And married."

Dorothy Boone sat still. "My mama went to New York for work after her husband died. She cleans house in Brooklyn. She took all the children up there but me. I was the oldest one, and I told her I could never like the city. So I stayed on. I got married right out of my grandparents' house. I was still young when they died."

The rocking started again, and her eyes moved away from mine. "I had eleven little children." Rock. "Three girls and four boys." Rock. "Livin'."

Her chair creaked to a stop. "We were working by the day. If you pick two hundred pounds of cotton, you're going to make two dollars. But, honey, it's gonna take you all day. If you pick only a hundred pounds, you don't get no two dollars. You get a dollar less, something like that.

"The highest I's picked is three hundred pounds a day. It hurts your back. I had one boy pick four hundred pounds of cotton." Rock. "One of them that died.

"Me and my boys shaked fifteen acres of peanuts and picked forty acres of cotton. Me and my children, we'd get paid twenty-five cents for a shock of peanuts. By myself in a day, I'd put up fifteen. But I add all the children, and we could sometimes put up two hundred shocks in a day."

Dorothy Boone started rocking again. "Now I just work in my garden. I plant peanuts. Beans. A patch of lettuce. I work until I'm fit to die. I wash and iron. By the time I pack my green beans, I don't want to do no more. I've done my share. I have done some work in my life.

"But my nerves are kinda bad. Women's change of life is tough on me. I reckon I worked hard. Now I do some day work some-times. Babysitting and housework. But they don't want to give you two dollars an hour for pay. They pay you what they want to. They pay you seventy-five cents if they can.

"Some things I remember, and I soon forget. My mama and daddy, they would tell us things. They always said, 'You don't remember it like we do. We worked for nothing.' You'd see them come in, tired from one day to another. It seems like so many days go by." She stopped rocking. "I don't see how in the world they lived, do you?

"You know, I wish they had told me more. Now my boy Melvin, he knows all about Roanoke Rapids. We didn't know nothing about it. Maybe Mama and Daddy knowed all about it and didn't tell us. He is dead and gone now. Yeah, that's just the way it is.

"We just didn't know nothing. We never did nothing but walk in the gutter. Maybe if they had told us, it'd been different.

"You know I was growed and married the first time I heard of Roanoke Rapids. I just first heard the name 'Stephenson' and about those mills when my boy went to work there. Right now if someone asked me, 'Where's your child workin' at?' I'd have to think before I could say, 'J. P. Stephenson.'

"When Melvin told me about the job he got, I told him, 'Well, you know you can't be going over there and messin' or the folks'll fire you and you're gonna have a bad name.' When he told me about the union, I told him, 'Melvin, you remember what you're doing. Don't get in there now and get yourself in trouble.' He said, 'Mama, I'm not going to bother nobody, but we want our rights. We wants to belong to the union.'

"Every one of my children, I tell them, you've got to work for eating. I have never had one minute's trouble with any of them. I have never had to get them out of jail or nothing like that. It seems just like they was always listening.

"One day I got kind of worried, thinking about Melvin and the union. I got to talking with an old schoolteacher of Melvin's, and I said, 'Somebody's gonna get on down the road and kill him.' She said to me, 'Ain't nobody gonna bother him, that Melvin.'

"All of them's growed, and they's on their own. And one thing. God helped me raise them, fix them so they know what they was doing and learn some sense and learn how to 'have themself.

"We didn't know nothing but just picking cotton, go home, wash out our clothes, iron, and clean the house up. That's all we learned about. Now I don't want to see Melvin work like I did. We couldn't never had done nothing like what Melvin done. A person now's gonna fight for their rights. Now Melvin, he's got something."

PART FIVE

The Company

The J. P. Stevens
Rule of Order

SHAREHOLDERS' MEETING

On March 2, 1977, the morning of the annual J. P. Stevens share-holders' meeting, a half-dozen Stevens workers from Roanoke Rapids, all white, flew to New York to parade "Stop the Boycott" signs outside the Union Square headquarters of the Amalgamated Clothing and Textile Workers Union. Their expenses were paid by the J. P. Stevens Employees Educational Committee, which had been formed in the autumn of 1976 for the purpose of oust-ing ACTWU from Roanoke Rapids and forcing a stop to the boycott of Stevens goods.

Uptown, by early afternoon three thousand demonstrators had ringed the Stevens Tower at Forty-sixth Street and the Avenue of the Americas in protest against the company's antiunion, anti-worker policies. Joining a delegation of pro-union J. P. Stevens workers parading outside their employer's headquarters were Paul O'Dwyer, president of the city council; Bella Abzug; Coretta Scott King; Bayard Rustin, executive director of the A. Philip Randolph Institute; representatives of the Seafarers Union, the United Federation of Teachers, Transportation Workers of Greater New York, Actors Equity, the Dining Room Employees Union, the International Ladies' Garment Workers Union, and the Federation of Catholic Teachers; members of the New York chapter of the National Organization for Women, the National

Lawyers Guild, and the Association of Legal Aid Attorneys; students from Columbia University, Rutgers, Yale, Princeton, and Wesleyan.

The group, bundled against the cold, marched around the building chanting "Boycott Stevens" and hoisting high banners and posters. One of the signs read, "Don't Sleep Tonight with J. P. Stevens: Boycott." Another said, "At J. P. Stevens: Profits First, People Last."

Lucy Taylor, who had traveled with a delegation of the CBLA to attend the shareholders' meeting, never intended to join the marchers outside. She simply did not have the strength. But she stood outside in the cold cheering them on for a few minutes. Then Cecil Jones, the ACTWU organizer, and Reverend Edward Fleming, a former Stevens worker from Roanoke Rapids, escorted her past the police line and guards. No sooner had Lucy gotten inside the Stevens Tower than she collapsed.

"I have to sit down. I just have to sit down," Lucy gasped.

Cecil asked the Stevens guards for a chair. They refused. Jones and Reverend Fleming helped Lucy into a bank off the lobby. An officer got her to a chair, and Lucy dug in her purse for her Schering 200 inhalator and put it in her mouth.

"Are you all right?" the banker asked.

"I just had to get my breath," Lucy said, her hand on her chest.

The banker, bewildered by her breathing attack, asked what was the matter with her.

She did not have enough breath to explain. Just then, outside the large windows a picket walked by carrying a poster of a big angry man with clumps and tangles of cotton covering his cap and shirt. Lucy pointed to it. "That's what I've got."

When she had caught her breath, she added, "That's Louis Harrell, bless his heart. He's been in and out of the hospital half a dozen times already this year. We worked together for Stevens."

"You mean this Stevens here?" the banker asked.

"That's the one," said Lucy. "It's working for them where I got like this. From breathing all their cotton dust."

When she was well enough to leave, she thanked the banker. Going back into the lobby of the Stevens Tower, she said, "They gave me brown lung, but I'm giving them hell."

Lucy Taylor, Cecil Jones, and Reverend Fleming found seats in the back row of the shareholders' meeting room on the second floor. They even had time to find Lucy a straight-back chair, easier for breathing than the soft armchairs provided.

Five hundred and fifty shareholders—many of them activists for corporate responsibility from church and union support groups—turned out for the annual meeting. They could not all be seated in the main meeting room. Two hundred of them were directed to the Andover Room and the Training Room, which Stevens personnel, nervously communicating with one another by walkie-talkie, referred to as "the overflow rooms."

In the Andover Room, "overflow shareholders" sat crammed together on folding metal chairs. They faced a blank wall and a microphone flanked by two dummies outfitted in clothes made of Stevens fabric. One mannequin had cropped blond hair and a plaid skirt; the other had sunglasses, a blazer, and trousers.

The color photograph of Board Chairman James D. Finley—jowly, bushy-eyebrowed, imperious—in the Stevens annual report and his voice—cultivated—descending from the ceiling speakers were all that connected the overflow shareholders to J. P. Stevens' chief executive officer, speaking in the main room.

Unseen and unseeing, the overflow shareholders listened to Finley's opening remarks. "Ladies and gentlemen, I am pleased to appear before you at another annual meeting of shareowners to review with you the operations of the Stevens Company during the past year. Much has been written and spoken about the union trying to unionize the Stevens Company and boycott its products, and the facts in many cases have been distorted and incorrectly reported. Our employees have rejected the union repeatedly, and in Roanoke Rapids, the one location where the union won its only election victory, a very large number of employees have joined together—without assistance of any kind from the company—for the purpose of getting rid of the union and ending the boycott."

"Dirty liar! You belong in jail!" someone shouted from the Andover Room. Muffled sounds of "Boycott Stevens!" "Boycott Stevens!" filtered into the main meeting room from outside the Stevens Tower, where demonstrators were still picketing.

"Two proposals for action at this meeting today were submitted by five religious organizations. One of the proposals deals directly with the company's labor-relations practices and policies. It is our feeling that these groups are made up of a relatively small number of individuals constituting a vocal minority not truly representative of the larger membership of the religious organizations for which they purport to speak. I say to all of these groups: Re-evaluate your position with the greatest possible objectivity. This is *not* a social cause. This is *not* a matter of economic justice.

"We do not claim to be perfect. We do not claim that we have always been right. There have been occasions when we made interpretations of the labor laws which we fully believed at the time to be correct, and the Labor Board later disagreed. We have made mistakes in the past. And we will probably make mistakes of judgment in the future.

"I stand before you today with a feeling of optimism and confidence in the future. Working together we can continue to produce results we will all be proud of."

The board of directors, their wives, Stevens executives, and some shareholders applauded Finley at the conclusion of his address. The majority was silent. Loud booing and hissing came from the overflow rooms. A shareholder tried to address the chairman.

"I'm asking you to hold your questions," Finley told him.

"No, no, Finley, it's not like in your mills," someone called out.

"You will have the right to speak at the meeting," Finley went on.

"Yeah, to the wall," said one of the shareholders in the Andover Room.

"This is my meeting. I'm running it," Finley said. "We didn't come here to debate anything. We came here to conduct the business of this meeting, which I intend to do."

A shareholder in the main meeting room politely asked, "By what rules do you conduct this meeting, by *Robert's Rules of Order?*"

"No," said Finley. "There are no rules."

An uproar among the shareholders.

"Now, listen, if you are going to misbehave now—"

More uproar.

"Now just be quiet now and sit down and behave. I can overrule anything. It's the J. P. Stevens rule of order here. That's the way we've been doing it for over 160 years."

A woman representative from the United Methodist Church tried to address Finley. "Mr. Chairperson," she began.

"Chairman, if you please."

Soon another voice was heard over the public address system. "Mr. Finley, I'm Reverend Edward Fleming from Roanoke Rapids. I'm a former employee of J. P. Stephenson. I've had a hard time with Stephenson."

Finley interrupted the black minister. "It's Stevens."

"Stevens," Reverend Fleming repeated, correcting himself. "I've had a hard time with Stevens. I started out in the dye plant working downstairs. At the time, all the blacks were downstairs, and all the whites were upstairs.

"I continued to press for a better job, but they did not give me a better job. What I'm saying is, I cannot see that this company really promotes blacks. Why can't blacks prosper in this company?"

James Finley had to wait for the applause for Reverend Fleming to die down.

Then Timothy Smith, the director of the Interfaith Center on Corporate Responsibility, sponsored by the National Council of Churches, addressed the chairman. "Mr. Finley, you know and I want our fellow shareholders to know that we have formally protested that you are misleading the shareholders here. You said in the proxy statement that 'It is management's belief that the resolutions [put forth by the five church organizations] were suggested by the Amalgamated Clothing and Textile Workers Union.' I would say, sir, that as soon as you say that to some shareholders, they're not going to support a request for an adjusted report. And further, I want to say that for six years, churches have been raising such resolutions with corporations.

"We do not need the help of any union to teach us how to put resolutions forward, to ask serious questions, to raise serious questions of corporate policy of companies. We have our own history. I want to put our position on the record: The company's statements are false and misleading. They make the vote null and invalid, and I would suggest that management should not vote its shares."

A nun in a white habit addressed the chairman. "Mr. Finley, my question is a very simple one. I have the right to know the truth, the full truth of your statement as you see it, and evidently your proxy statements are only half of what you see. I feel you owe it to me and to your other stockholders who came here to vote to have that information available prior to the election if the election is more than some kind of rubber stamp."

"I accept your statement, but I disagree," Finley responded. "I do not agree because what we have done is perfectly legal, right, moral, and everything else. We do not feel the unions are necessary. We feel like we do not need a third party between our people and us. We've consistently said this. We're going to work along those lines."

"Mr. Finley," said another shareholder. "My name is Bob Hall, from Chapel Hill, North Carolina. I was here last year with a proposal. I did a real quick check the other day of J. P. Stevens stock compared with five or six other textile companies, and J. P. Stevens stock was going down while other textile companies were holding their own or going up slightly. That indicated something to me, that there was some difference in the effect of the market on J. P. Stevens.

"Investors have to make the decision as to whether they think they should invest in a company that is taking the kind of actions you are or whether they should put their money in some other company that is not involved in such controversial issues."

Finley looked chagrined and scratched his head.

A woman stood at the floor microphone waiting to speak. "My name is Coretta Scott King, and I'm from Atlanta, Georgia."

Most of the shareholders—not the Stevens board, or the executives, or their wives—rose to their feet to give Mrs. King a long ovation.

"Mr. Chairman, ladies and gentlemen, I come before you as a representative of a body of concerned stockholders and as an American intolerant of injustice. Both the pangs of the struggle to end discrimination in the place of employment and the pangs of the struggle for a more abundant life have been frequent visitors to my home.

"I would like to call your attention to a prophetic comment of my late husband at the height of the Montgomery bus protest. In 1956 he said, 'Our struggle is not toward putting the bus company out of business, but toward putting justice in business.'

"The people who work at the Stevens Company have used lawful nonviolence and lawful channels for expressing their grievances against the Stevens Company, which has been found by administrative bodies guilty of labor law violations on a number of occasions. I call upon you to join me in voting for these resolutions, which if adopted will vindicate the stand taken by working people who want to have a better life and make Stevens a better company. In closing, may I say, an abundant and secure life is unattainable for working people except through trade unions of their own choosing."

Shouts of "Right on!" came from the overflow rooms, and the applause for Mrs. King was prolonged.

In the last row of the main meeting room, Lucy Taylor pulled herself out of her chair and slowly made her way to one of the microphones. "Mr. Finley, I have a breathing condition that two doctors have said is byssinosis. Now one time, back when I was able to work in the mill, two looms next to me caught fire. I could not catch my breath, so I went to stand at the door to breathe. The supervisor came and asked me why I left my job. I told him I just couldn't breathe with all that smoke. He said, 'Get back on the job. Machinery costs money.' The company considers that machinery is the most important thing. That's the way Stevens handles their labor relations, making machinery more important than people.

"I was fourteen when I started working in the mills, and thirty-six years laboring in the mills makes me an expert on labor relations. We have nothing. We work to do the best we can. Stevens has a labor policy that is criminal."

James Finley peered over the top of his reading glasses at the shareholders applauding for Lucy Taylor. The year before, at the 1976 Stevens shareholder meeting, Thomas ("Buck") Malone, a disabled worker and colleague of Lucy Taylor's in the Roanoke Rapids chapter of the CBLA, had mustered his courage to stand and say, "When I retired, all I got from J. P. Stevens was $1,500, a plaque, and a case of brown lung." Finley had looked at the old man and said, "Byssinosis is something that is alleged to come from cotton dust. It is a word that's been coined, but it has no meaning." During the year, both the CBLA and the ACTWU had grown in support and strength. Finley knew better than to repeat his allegation.

"I've got a question," Lucy said to the board chairman.

"Yes, ma'am?"

"When I was born in Roanoke Rapids, the mills were run and owned by Samuel Finley Patterson, one of the most wonderful men I have ever known. You have the name Finley too. I just wondered if you have the wonderful traits he had."

Finley looked pleased. "Well, I hope so, the way you describe him. I hope I do."

Lucy walked out of range of the microphone, her back to the chairman, and added, "Well, I can't see them."

Another former J. P. Stevens worker stepped to the microphone. This black man had worked as a supply clerk at Stevens' Montgomery, Alabama, plant until he was fired after signing a union card.

"Mr. Finley, my name is Reverend Alvin Pinkard. I came to J. P. Stevens five years ago with a business degree. I've been to our state university. I was promised a position with the company. I came there with some fine experience from another textile plant. Yet every time an opening came up for a supervisor's job, I always trained the man to be my supervisor. And I always asked the question, 'Why? Why not me?' They'd say, 'You're not ready.'

"If I'm not ready to run the job, how can I train another man to run the job? Also, you stated that the majority of J. P. Stevens workers do not want a union. If this is the case, why does your company continue brutalizing people who want a union?"

"How many questions are you going to put in this one question?"

"You're a smart man. You can take two questions at a time."

"It is our policy, as a matter of fact, to promote from within the company with the people we have without regard to race, creed, or anything else," Finley said. "We try to do this. We've made some, ah, misjudgments along the way. I think I said in my speech, we are subject to misjudgments."

"Well, now, you know and I know that that has not been the policy. You're the top executive. I say, why not find out."

A shareholder whispered to his companion, "He's got Finley on the run now."

"I have no way of knowing about things of that type. It's just impossible for me to know."

"Are you saying that you are not aware of the fact that your plants are discriminating against blacks?"

"With twenty-five hundred people, I mean, I don't know how in the world I could know about everything that goes on," Finley said, flustered into forgetting that Stevens employed 45,000 people.

"Well now you know. And the board of directors, I'm sure, would like to know what is going on—"

Finley cut off Reverend Pinkard. "No, the answer to that—"

"You say it is the company policy."

"That's right," Finley said.

"For all these years, man, no black has been promoted. If you are the chairman, why not investigate the matter if you are concerned about it."

"Well, sir, we are concerned about it, as a matter of fact. We do live up to the law. We've made mistakes, and the policy of this company is as I put forth to you before: We have never asked anyone, we have never approved or condoned anyone disobeying the law of the land, or any state or local law or federal law. I told you, we've made errors. We admit that. I don't deny that."

"If you were chairman of my company, and you did not know what was going on in the company," Pinkard said, "I'd suggest we get a new chairman." Many of the shareholder-activists broke into long applause.

Congress Comes to Town

HEARINGS ON LABOR LAW REFORM

Workers from all over the South crowded into the Roanoke Rapids Civic Center on August 9, 1977, for the congressional field hearings on national labor law reform. Some were J. P. Stevens workers; others were employees of other antilabor companies. The hearings were being held in Roanoke Rapids because of the major role in southern antiunionism of the largest employer in town. Yet glaring in its absence was the key witness: J. P. Stevens and Company.

"We come to Roanoke Rapids, North Carolina, with a great sense of anticipation, but also a bit of disappointment," Frank Thompson, Jr., of New Jersey, chairman of the House Subcommittee on Labor-Management Relations, began. "My disappointment arises from the refusal of any management representatives themselves to appear before our subcommittee.

"We sent specific invitations to James Finley, chairman of the board of J. P. Stevens, and to the heads of five other major area corporations which have been the target of criticism before our subcommittee in recent years. We invited Deering Milliken, Florida Steel, Monroe Auto Equipment, Dow Chemical, and Litton Industries, offering them an opportunity to respond to the testimony about their labor relations practices. None of them has accepted those invitations, and that I deeply regret."

The rank-and-file union negotiating committee sat shoulder to shoulder. James Boone, Carolyn Brown, Maurine Hedgepeth,

Bennett Taylor, Raymond Hollowell, Joyce Bush, Danny Black-
well, the others. They wore paper Liberty Bells reading, "I'm a
Stevens worker. I support labor law reform." They had insisted on
being let off work for the occasion, and their concerted demand
was met.

Members of the CBLA were there. Louis Harrell, out of his
sick bed and taking part in an action for the first time in over a
year, sat next to the union negotiating committee, with his wife,
Lillian, at his side. A few rows back, F. K. Taylor had his arm
around Lucy.

Already seated at the witness table were ACTWU's William
DuChessi, executive vice-president; Jacob Sheinkman, secretary-
treasurer; Arthur Goldberg, general counsel; Paul Swaity, director
of organization; Scott Hoyman, vice-president and southern regional director; Joel Ax, associate general counsel, and Nicholas
Zonarich, director of organization for the AFL-CIO's Industrial
Union Department.

William DuChessi pushed his glasses to the top of his head and
propped his bare elbows on the witness table. J. P. Stevens
"doesn't have the *guts* to testify before this committee. It will not
meet with a reporter. It won't even give the courtesy to this committee of appearing before it.

"Last night," DuChessi said, "a local Stevens official walked
into the lobby of one of the motels in this city and gave a bellhop
over there seventeen or eighteen brochures with a list of rooms in
which people were staying and told this bellhop, 'Would you
please see to it that one of these is stuck under the doors of every
one of these rooms.' It is quite a brochure. What audacity, not to
want to face this committee, and then throw this canned baloney
at the media and at this committee."

"I happened to be in my room at the time last night when
those rounds were being made," Congressman Ted Weiss of New
York added. "The door was pounded on. I thought it was going to
be broken down. I asked who it was. I got no response at all.
Then there was the pounding again. I finally opened the door.
Somebody was there to give me a packet of J. P. Stevens material.
I assume if this is the kind of subtlety they use on a member of
Congress, I can just imagine what their other tactics must be
like."

"Well," Chairman Frank Thompson said, "I and a number of others were paid guests at the Holiday Inn last night. In the absence of a number of us from our rooms, this document was not put under the door. Rather, the door was opened, and the document was placed inside the room. Where I come from"—Thompson paused—"that would be breaking and entering."

Then Jacob Sheinkman spoke. "We all know that the National Labor Relations Act guarantees workers the right to choose freely their representatives and to bargain collectively with employers over wages, fringe benefits, and working conditions. That's the law. It has been upheld by the courts. But no one in this room needs to be told that it has been turned into a cruel farce, here and in other areas where nonunion employers have entrenched themselves. Consider just one example—the J. P. Stevens Company.

"Here in Roanoke Rapids, J. P. Stevens, that billion-dollar multinational corporation has for three years ignored its legal obligation to bargain in good faith. It has turned negotiations into an ugly, frustrating charade. And what has the government done about this flouting of the law? I'll tell you. It has over the years awarded J. P. Stevens tens of millions of dollars in textile contracts. Just this last week it was awarded a $3.4-million contract by the Defense Logistics Agency. In effect, our government is condoning J. P. Stevens' violations of federal law. Even worse, it is continuing to reward those violations. We are asking for a basic reform of the National Labor Reform Act."

Paul Swaity introduced two J. P. Stevens workers from the West Boylston plant in Montgomery, Alabama—Jerry Davis and Louise Bailey.

Davis, who is young and black, spoke first. "I am a Stevens worker—at least I was when I left. The way they have been firing people back in Montgomery, you cannot be sure about your job if you're strong union. The campaign started in July. Just as soon as the company saw how many people were signing cards, they started doing whatever they could do to scare us off. In August they started firing union supporters. Eleven union members were fired in the first few months of our campaign. Now those are just the people that the Labor Board said were illegal discharges. More union supporters have been fired since then. Two more of us were fired last week. We all feel like we might be next. How can you buy anything on time, or make any plans for the future with that kind of fear? But that fear is the J. P. Stevens way of fighting the union.

"The company tried to scare us by holding meetings in the plant. They made us cut off our spinning frames and made us go to the meetings where they told us if we signed union cards all the cards would be put on the courtroom table and then the company would know who all had signed.

"That didn't stop us, but it made a lot of people worried about going to a union meeting. And it made people who were thinking about signing cards a lot less willing to sign them. I think Stevens shouldn't be allowed to scare people like they do."

Then Louise Bailey, who had been a spinner in the West Boylston plant for thirty-six years, addressed the congressmen. "Back in the forties we had a CIO union, and we were going real well, real well. Then all of a sudden, no orders. They shut the plant down. We were all laid off. In about three months they begin to call back all nonunion hands but very few union hands. I know that for a fact. I was there. For four years I didn't work. I know what it is to go hungry. I know what it is when you have a child."

Maurine Hedgepeth listened carefully to the white Montgomery woman, for this was her story too, being kept out of work for four years for union activities.

"When I would go to a place for a job and they asked, 'Where did you work last?' all I had to say was 'West Boylston.' Right then they said, 'Union.' And I never got a job.

"When the case came up four years later, they made them put me back to work. We got the worst job in the mill. They never let us forget that we was had to be put back there. Now, listen. I am scared every day I go in that plant because I am a strong union worker. I wonder a lot of times, will I be the next union member to get fired? I feel just sick to my gut because when I go in there now, you know, I don't know whether I am going to have a job or not.

"And I feel guilty of these that have been laid off because I was one of the strong union workers that has got these people to sign up. They come to me because I'm an old hand. They just come to me and ask me, 'What do you think?' I said, 'It's the best thing that ever happened here.'

"You congressmen have it in your power to make things the way it should be, to help us to help ourselves and our children and our children's children, to be there when we are dead and gone. We are not asking for the world, but just a chance to hold our head up. As God has been good to us, let us be good to others. I hope you can teach that lesson to J. P. Stevens before they fire another one of our workers."

When Louise Bailey finished her testimony, Paul Swaity addressed the congressional panel. "In terms of the delays, there is certainly no better illustration of the injustice that workers suffer than those who have suffered from the Darlington plant. I would like, with your permission, Mr. Chairman, to recognize those workers and have them stand up. They have come a long distance."

All eyes were on the eight old men and women in the second row, former workers at the Darlington Manufacturing Company, a wholly-owned subsidiary of the Deering Milliken Company, which was controlled by the Milliken family. On September 6, 1956, they had voted for union representation.

The day after the union victory Roger Milliken, president of the Darlington, South Carolina, plant and all but one of Deering Milliken's chain of twenty-seven textile mills, made good his pre-election threat by deciding to shut down his Darlington plant. Milliken's decision became public after it was approved at a special meeting of the board of directors held six days after the union victory.

A petition was circulated in the Darlington plant in the presence of supervisory personnel. Eighty-three per cent of the 550 Darlington workers signed it, stating that they would withdraw from the union if management reversed its decision to close the plant. In response, Milliken announced, "As long as there are 17 per cent of these hard-core labor people here, I refuse to run the mill."

In November 1956 the mill ceased operation and all the workers were terminated. Milliken sold the mill piecemeal at auction, despite the consideration of various members of the board of directors that the plant could continue to be operated as a profit-making enterprise. Milliken wanted it dismantled as quickly as possible to let the "lesson" of Darlington permeate his chain of mills.

In March 1965, nearly ten years later, the Supreme Court ruled that it was legal for an employer to close down its *entire* business, even if this was done because the employees had formed a union. However, the Court held, a partial closing is an unfair labor practice if it is motivated by an intent to "chill unionism" in the employer's other plants.

At this time, more than twenty years after the mill was shut down, more than twelve years after the Supreme Court decision, ten years after the U. S. Fourth Circuit Court of Appeals upheld the National Labor Relations Board ruling that the Darlington workers were entitled to back pay and reinstatement at other Milliken mills, the Milliken Company has not rehired a single Darlington worker nor paid one penny in back wages. One-third of the workers have died; many more moved away in search of work.

Next, Scott Hoyman introduced the panel of J. P. Stevens workers from Roanoke Rapids. Louis Harrell went to the witness table.

"I have been in this work all my life until my breathing kept getting worse and worse. I finally had to quit. If we had some good laws that made the company come across, they couldn't have kept me in that dust that long because that was making me sick. If we had some good laws on the books and had arbitration of grievances, we might have gotten those things straightened out, and I could have got out of the dust and probably been working now."

Chairman Thompson strained to hear Harrell's barely audible voice. "They don't try to help nobody. You work your life away up there and all they do is sit back and laugh at you for being sick, write up personnel reports for being out when you are under a doctor's care.

"So if there is any way we can get some laws to help us out in union activity here and help make them come across with a contract so we can get some laws for health. You may think this is funny, but it is not. This hurts."

When Harrell finished talking, Congressman John M. Ashbrook of Ohio, the only Republican on the subcommittee, caught Jacob Sheinkman's eye and held it in his gaze.

"I assume you are an attorney, are you not?"

"Excuse me?" said Sheinkman, startled.

"You are an attorney?"

"I am."

"I would expect an attorney to present one side," Ashbrook said. "I don't think there is anything wrong with that. It is a pretty one-sided case that you are presenting, although I am not so sure the facts are one-sided. We have wandered all over. We have really come down here on legislation, and it sounds more like a hanging match at this point."

Congressman Dale E. Kildee of Michigan interjected, "I would submit to my colleague from Ohio that if it is one-sided, it is because J. P. Stevens has chosen not to attend here this morning. You know, what is happening here in Roanoke Rapids seems to be a rerun of what was happening in my home town of Flint, Michigan, in the mid-1930s. Every attempt was made to keep the unions from organizing in the mid-1930s. But they finally won a contract in 1937, two years after the passage of the Wagner Act, the National Labor Relations Act.

"And here I come to Roanoke Rapids and find a rerun, kind of a déjà vu, of what I experienced when I was about seven years old and what my father experienced forty years ago in Flint, Michigan. One would think that the law would have solved some of these problems in that time.

"You know, during those days, I can recall vividly, just about the time I made my first Holy Communion, the terrible conditions in the plant at that time. And they also had Pinkerton detectives and undercover people following my father's co-workers, the organizers especially."

"We used to have that in days gone by," said ACTWU's DuChessi, who had started out at age fourteen as a carpet worker in Amsterdam, New York. "We were chased out of town and threatened to get out of town or else. The record is full of that. But in recent years employers are more subtle. They hire these high-class public relations guys and high-class law firms who know all of the ins and outs of how to bust the law, and then stonewall it, like this company has done. It is more sophisticated today.

"But they do other things," DuChessi said. "It is no secret. The wiretaps. It puts the union meetings under surveillance. It quizzes union members as to who went to a meeting. There are foremen from time to time outside of a hall where we are holding a meeting or a parking lot counting who is going in. That is still taking place."

Frank Thompson listened attentively, then spoke. "The chair has just one comment relating to violence. I deplore it. I went all through the Landrum-Griffin fight in 1959." That fight was over a controversial amendment to the Labor Act which, among other things, limited the right of unions to picket during organizing drives. During that legislation, Frank Thompson firmly opposed any curtailment of workers rights.

"I was subjected to violence right in the middle of the conference on that legislation," Thompson said, "when I was sprayed by unknown persons with sulphuric acid. I don't think things like that happen much any more. I pray and hope they never do again."

"I would like to bring a witness here at this particular moment," said Jacob Sheinkman. "An incident arose last week which I think this committee should hear about. And I would like him to tell it because it bears on the use of potential violence."

A blond, blue-eyed young man addressed the panel of congressmen. "My name is Tommy Boroughs. I went to work for J. P. Stevens in Aberdeen, South Carolina, two weeks after I come back from Vietnam. Since 1973, when we started a campaign down there, I have been handing out leaflets and doing whatever I could to help.

"A week ago today we were going to hand out a leaflet at four o'clock in the evening, before going to work. It was raining, so we decided to wait until after shift change, twelve o'clock midnight.

"At that time, I went through the gate, and I got out of my car. I was passing out leaflets. Traffic was trying to come out of the mill pretty fast. Traffic was backed up on the highway about a hundred yards. So I decided I would go back through the gate, passing out literature to the people in the cars. The gate guard said, 'You can't pass out that stuff over here. Get behind the gate.' So I turned around. I went out through the gate. I told the union organizer that he told me to get out, and I couldn't do it over there. She said, 'You have a right to do it. Go back over there.' So I did.

"At that time he scared the hell out of me. He pulled a pistol out. He went to his truck, come around there. I was still passing out literature. He told me, he said, 'Tommy, I'm not going to tell you again. Get behind that damned gate.' I went behind the gate."

"I would have gone under it, I think," Thompson said.

"To tell you the truth, I'm still scared," Boroughs added.

"Well, I hope that threat is never carried out," Thompson said softly.

The next witnesses were legislators, State Senator William Smith and State Representative Thomas B. Sawyer.

The representative grinned at the committee. "My name is Tom Sawyer. I guess a name like that does help you get elected." Then he addressed Chairman Thompson. "You have brought this committee to an antiunion state. North Carolina has the lowest percentage of organized workers of any state in the union, and far too many of our leaders, both political and industrial, find it profitable to maintain the status quo.

"Let me give you an illustration that occurred less than two weeks ago. The Brockway Glass Company, a large manufacturer with eighteen plants nationwide, was considering locating a new plant near Roxboro, North Carolina, not too far from here, in Person County. The new plant would have eventually employed seventeen hundred workers at wages above the four dollars per hour rate.

"The Person County Industrial Development Commission, dominated by local industrialists, voted to issue a qualified invitation to the company if they would do two things—come here nonunion and stay that way, and pay prevailing wages in the county instead of the proposed four dollars per hour minimum.

"The chairman of the commission had the audacity to speak for the workers in that area when he said, 'We have a history of nonunion industry around here, and our labor force doesn't think union. We feel that we really don't have any place for unions here, and we feel an obligation to the industries already here to

protect them from unionization.' Case after case of this sort of
thing has come to light recently.

"Xerox was kept out of the Research Triangle. Sylvania was
kept out of Smithfield. Miller Beer was kept out of Raleigh. And
that is just the tip of the iceberg. Those are the ones that we
found out about.

"Mr. Chairman, these are the kind of industrial nightriders
and vigilantes that conspire to keep workers down throughout this
state. What does all this mean? It means that in many cases that
the entire power structure of a community conspires to frustrate
his or her rights to union representation."

State Senator Smith spoke briefly. "You know the old biblical
quotation that 'I will lift up my eyes unto the hills from whence
cometh my help.' Well, the working people in North Carolina
will have to lift up their eyes to you if they expect any help, because they are not going to get it from the government of North
Carolina."

Chairman Thompson looked at the legislators. "Thank you
very much, Senator and Mr. Sawyer. I realize, in light of the prevailing attitude in this state, it takes a considerable amount of
courage for you two distinguished gentlemen to appear before us."

A panel of representatives from Southerners for Economic Justice, a nonprofit organization based in Chapel Hill, North Carolina, testified before the hearing. The executive director, Bill
Finger, addressed the congressmen. "We see economic justice as
the most critical issue before our country for the next decade. We
feel it critical to come to terms with both the symbol of J. P.
Stevens and the details of what is going on with the J. P. Stevens
Company."

Diana Wilson, the young, black assistant director, said, "People's concerns with union campaigns today are like what black
Southerners experienced during the early civil rights days. The
laws are not strong enough to protect us. For any kind of movement it takes people to start it, to get the momentum going. This
movement to fight the injustices experienced by southern workers
has the people. Now it needs the laws."

Rev. W. W. Finlator, a member of the board of the organization, continued, "Those of us who have lived always in the
South have come to believe that our southern land which we love

so much has in fact become a colonial possession of the other parts of the country. People have come in and exploited our people. This must come to an end."

A panel of members of the J. P. Stevens Employees Educational Committee were introduced, together with the committee's counsel, Robert Valois, and his law partner, Frank Ward, Jr.

"Do you have prepared statements?" Thompson asked.

"We do," said Valois. "I would just like to take this opportunity to make a couple of remarks concerning some of the earlier testimony. I came here with the idea that the union would be allotted a substantial amount of time, and that certainly has been so.

"I regret there is not a spokesman here, other spokesmen here, from industry. We do not speak for industry. I represent individual employees who are seeking to get out from under a union they don't wish to have. The J. P. Stevens Employees Educational Committee is composed of employees who do not desire to be represented by the union certified by the NLRB to represent them."

"It is my understanding that several months ago five members of your committee went to New York to picket the ACTWU headquarters. Who paid for that trip?" Thompson asked.

"The committee paid for it with its own funds," Valois answered.

"Where are the committee's funds derived?"

"From the public."

"All from the public?"

"That is correct."

"And what do you mean by 'the public'?" Thompson questioned.

"From individuals across the United States," Valois answered.

"None from the textile industry?"

"None from J. P. Stevens Company."

"Other textile industries?" Thompson prodded. "Any other textile industries?"

"Frankly, I don't have a list of contributors with me. I think that we have gotten some support from the textile industry."

"What is your annual budget?"

"We don't have one established."

"What percentage of your budget would you estimate comes from Stevens workers themselves?"

"I really don't know."

"I see," said Thompson. "Well, now, your Educational Committee has solicited contributions?"

"That is correct," conceded Valois.

"Through ads in the American Textile Manufacturers Institute publications and other industry and trade journals. What percentage of your finances come from the textile industry, do you know?"

"I really don't know."

Congressman Ted Weiss picked up the questioning. "Were you involved with the formation of the J. P. Stevens Employees Educational Committee?"

"Well, I suppose so, yes."

"When was that formed?"

"About a year ago."

"And were you retained by the organization after it was formed or were you involved in the formation itself?"

"After, I suppose."

"Well, would you tell me that you were involved in the formation of it or were you involved after?"

"Well, I believe it is after. But I don't know how that is pertinent, really."

"And do you know at this point what the annual cost of running the association is?"

"I don't know that."

"Do you have papers of association or incorporation?"

"Yes."

"Did you draw that up?"

"No."

"Do you know who did?"

"Yes."

"Who did?"

"One of my law partners."

"I see I have to be more precise with my questions," Weiss said. "Was it your law firm that drew up the papers?"

"Yes."

"Do you know who keeps the records of expenditures of the committee?"

"I don't think that this is pertinent, frankly," Valois said. "I'm afraid that I would be going beyond my scope of my testimony here and invade a privilege of my clients."

"Well, of course you have the right to answer or not answer the questions in any fashion at all. However, I would be interested to know whether in fact we have a strictly independent committee," Weiss said.

"I can assure you we do. If that is where the questions are leading, the answer to that question is yes."

"How much of your monies comes from employees as compared to how much of it comes from nonemployees?"

"I really don't know the answer to the question."

"Can you tell me the average amount that you spent last year, the total amount the committee spent last year? Was it ten thousand dollars, a hundred thousand dollars, a million dollars? Do you have any idea at all?"

"I don't want to get into that."

"Well, could you tell me how many employees the committee has, paid employees?"

"None."

"Could you tell us how much your firm is paid?"

"No."

"Is the firm paid anything at all?"

"I don't want to get into that. That, if you please, gets into lawyer-client matters which I don't think are matters of public interest."

"Well, I must tell you," Weiss said, "I would be interested in knowing whether in fact you are a tool of J. P. Stevens and Company or not."

"The answer to your question is that we are not."

Representative Weiss persisted. "Are there dues that are paid by the individual members of the Educational Committee?"

"I don't want to get into the finances."

"Okay. If you are willing to let that record stand, I am."

"I am willing to let the record stand the way it is." Valois said before introducing Leonard Curtis Wilson, Educational Committee member and the husband of Lucy Taylor's niece, Eloise.

"Mr. Chairman, I attended a funeral of my brother in Massachusetts just a few weeks ago," Wilson began. "I came by that great town of Lawrence, Massachusetts. I came by the river of Lawrence, and I saw all the closed textile mills there. I talked to a lot of people there in the town. Before the union came to Lawrence, there were twenty shoe factories there. There is only two in operation now. It is my opinion that the union will destroy anything that it cannot control."

Weiss studied Wilson. "Are you aware of the fact that the reason that many of those plants were closed down is because the employers, the mill owners, found that they could in fact go someplace else in this country and undercut by a half or as little as a third of what they were paying the employees in Lawrence?"

"Well, maybe so, sir," said Wilson. "We have some of those down here in the South, I am quite sure."

"Mr. Wilson, if you will, let me ask you this question: What is the hourly wage that the average employee earns at your company?"

"I can only tell you mine. Mine is $5.12 per hour."

The Roanoke Rapids union members whistled and hooted. One called out, "Pet! Bossman's pet!" The Stevens workers knew, although Weiss might not, that the loom fixer's job is the most prestigious, the highest paid in the mill-worker echelon, and that Wilson's wage was considerably higher than average.

"How many loom fixers are there?" Weiss asked.

"In the particular mill I work in, there is only six per shift, which is a total of eighteen."

"Okay. Supposing, Mr. Wilson, that the J. P. Stevens Company discovered that they could move to some town in South Carolina and pay loom fixers only $2.20 an hour instead of the $5.00 that you earn, and the other employees as well maybe a half or a third as much of what they are paying your fellow employees. Do you think that would be okay for J. P. Stevens to do that?"

"No, I don't think—"

"You don't think it would be okay?"

"No."

"Would you think it was not okay for J. P. Stevens to move out of Lawrence, Massachusetts, because they could get people to work more cheaply someplace else?"

"I would like you to repeat that, what you said."

"What I said was, do you think that it was okay for people like J. P. Stevens to move out of Lawrence, Massachusetts, because they could move into nonorganized, non-union-organized areas, and pay their new employees a half or a third as much as what they were paying in Lawrence, Massachusetts? You think that is okay?"

"If the people were willing to work for it, yes."

"And how about the people who had been working for them in Lawrence, Massachusetts?"

"Those people are without jobs now."

"That is right," said Weiss. "And do you think that that was the fault of the unions or people like J. P. Stevens?"

"Well," Wilson answered, "according to the Chamber of Commerce, sir, they said it was for economic reasons."

"Mr. Wilson, do you believe that the laborer is worthy of his hire?"

"I believe any man deserves what he earns, he or she, no more and no less. I don't believe they should be promised more than they earn."

Wilson addressed Frank Thompson. "Mr. Chairman, a few years ago the AFL-CIO union sent its organizers to Roanoke Rapids. They brought their propaganda material and passed it out to anyone who would accept it. They promised us a new way of life if we would sign the blue union card and vote the union in.

"They promised us almost a new world to live in, such as more money per hour for our work, better working conditions, better insurance, better retirement, more paid holidays. A lot of people did believe the union's promises and they voted the union in.

"But we do not think it fair to God and our country for the unions to insist on raising the prices of everything that is made or growed by escalating the price of labor and making the promise of more and more money each year when an apple today is worth no more than an apple the same size and quality a year ago, or even fifty years ago.

"I do believe it is against God's will for the unions to preach more and more money, for First Timothy 6:10 tells us that the love of money is the root of all evil.

"I do believe the union is a tool of the Devil bringing on the mark of the Beast. Revelations 1:5 tells us before the end of time the ones here on earth must have the mark to buy or sell. I do believe it is time to put God back into everything we do and honor the counsel of Jesus Christ when he said we can serve but one master. I thank you people for allowing God into this building today."

Frank Thompson addressed Wilson. "I wonder if God meant that that one master had to be J. P. Stevens."

"Sir, I think I should have a chance to answer that," Wilson said. "He meant money. Christ said that that was money."

"Yes," said Thompson. "I don't know whether, however, he was so specific as to peg it at $1.75 less than the rest of the nation."

A few moments later, however, acknowledging that his agile wit was as regional a characteristic as Wilson's Bible-quoting, Thompson turned to the Stevens worker again. "Before calling on others for questions, I would like to say to you, sir, that I meant no deprecation of your religious convictions at all. I have deep respect for your opinion that you would rather not be union. That is really what this is all about, to give workers their free choice, where a majority rules, as to whether there will be a union or not."

Wilbur Hobby, president of the North Carolina state AFL-CIO, went to the witness table. "I would like to make a comment. Mr. Valois got up here and he talked and represented this group, and that is his right, as it is my right to be here today.

"This is not the first time he has worked to decertify the trade union movement, where the people have voted. He was successful in a large plant in Raleigh, North Carolina, a couple of years ago, named Rockwell. And the law firm which he comes out of, one of the senior law partners, Tom Ellis, was the campaign manager for the Republican senator from this state, a fellow by the name of Jesse Helms, who has used his stationery, his letterheads, to send out over ten million pieces of literature for an organization called Americans United Against Union Control of the Government.

"And we find this reprehensible, that a man representing any state uses that kind of influence, the stationery of the United States Senate, to send out ten million pieces of literature with the most biased poll that you have ever seen. His questions are so biased, even I have to answer with a 'yes' because I wouldn't want what he threatened to happen to this country."

Congressman Weiss addressed the workers in the room: "The fight that you are waging here in North Carolina and the rest of the South is not just your fight for the workers down here. In New York City, where I come from, we have lost literally hundreds of thousands of jobs where the company simply picked up and moved to areas where there is no union organization.

"So you are really fighting the oppression not just of your workers, potential or actual, but also for the jobs that people in the industrialized and organized areas of the country, where people are losing their jobs, hand over fist, because they are running away to places that don't have union organization. It seems to me you ought not to be waging that fight with your hands tied behind your back. And that is really what this hearing is all about."

"Changes are coming about, I am almost certain," Chairman Thompson said. "It is inevitable. It is just a question of time."

"Let me ask just one simple, somewhat rhetorical question, and any of you may answer it," Representative Kildee said. "If the federal Congress does not act on labor law reform, how long do you think we have to wait to achieve a measure of justice from the Assembly of North Carolina?"

Wilbur Hobby attempted an answer. "We in the South—labor, management, government, and in fact all of our citizens—must take a good look at where we are at and where we want to go. We do not need another period of the robber barons to develop the great potential in the South.

"Congressman Kildee asked the question, if this committee doesn't act on labor law reform, how long will it take before these injustices are corrected? And I would like to tell you how long it will be in a very brief statement: until eternity or the revolution comes. And if we don't have some corrections, I think maybe that revolution might come."

Maybe They Can Do Something About It

EARL AND VIRGINIA DAVIS

Lewis Edwards' wife, Shelby Davis Edwards, was at the ACTWU local on Roanoke Avenue. Just after four o'clock shift change, a nearly steady stream of Stevens workers had come in with complaints about the company. Shelby had come from the Fabricating Plant, where she worked as a bar tacker, sewing labels in terry towels. Her hair, glasses, face, shirt, slacks, and shoes were covered with lint. She fingered two J. P. Stevens labels as she talked to Cecil Jones.

"Look at these labels. Anyone can see the new ones are nearly twice the size of the old. We can't do them in the same amount of time. The new beach towels we're working on are half again as long as the old ones. They're so long they don't lie on our tables straight. It takes longer. Now, I've been working there nine years, and it's hard to make production on these new towels. We're losing money."

Jones listened as Shelby Edwards continued. "And another thing. They've laid off the second shift of bar tackers and part of the first. That's left five of us bar tacking. They keep asking us to work overtime, but nobody will when they've got people laid off. I believe there's no point in grumbling if it's not going to get you nowhere. There's no point in complaining unless you're going to stand up for yourself and get something done about it."

PART SIX

The Union

Clyde Bush, the silver-haired chief textile-union organizer in Roanoke Rapids, sitting nearby, overheard Shelby. "This is the first time in the history of the J. P. Stevens Company that their workers have been able to make management listen to their problems.

"We carry the workers into the Potato House to grievance meetings with the company. We can carry in anybody we want to. They see for themselves how the company treats people. That builds strength for the union."

Shortly after the union won representation rights in Roanoke Rapids in 1974, J. P. Stevens agreed to a union proposal for a grievance procedure in which company and union would meet outside formal contract negotiations. At the meetings, the company was to keep the union posted on day-to-day operational changes in the Roanoke Rapids plants, and the union had the right to raise grievances about these changes and the discipline and discharge of employees.

When the grievance procedure was established in 1974, it had seemed a hopeful sign. Optimism waned when Stevens appointed Tommy Gardner to act on its behalf in the grievance meetings. The Second Circuit Court of Appeals had found Gardner in contempt for his involvement in unfair labor practices in Roanoke Rapids. Later Gardner was replaced by Roger Warren, who had never worked in the mills before he was hired by Stevens to represent the company in these meetings with the union.

Between September 1974 and March 1977 alone, Bush and Jones accompanied Stevens employees who had grievances to 209 meetings with the Stevens representatives. The company did not change its mind about one of the five hundred instances of proposed discharge or discipline. Still, establishing a mechanism for processing grievances was a small step forward. The repeated challenges to the company forced Stevens to explain how it made personnel decisions and produced greater consistency in its policy guidelines.

Cecil Jones, who had been the first black president of his textile-union local in Fredericksburg, Virginia, before he came to Roanoke Rapids, said, "We've had a lot of people walk into our office and say, 'I was opposed to the union on election day, and I still am.' But they've got a grievance, and they bring it to us."

Shelby Edwards said that her mother, Virginia Davis, was one of those who had come to the union with a complaint about the company. Then she told me her parents were fiercely antiunion, that they had been scabs in a past textile strike, and they were afraid of the company.

Shelby said her parents would never talk with me. But mother and daughter talked on the telephone every day, and after a week Shelby's mother got curious. One day Shelby said that her mother wouldn't "mind" if I talked to her.

Virginia Davis came to the front door of her house, five blocks from the Patterson Mill. She was a thin woman with short, curled, reddish hair and gold-framed glasses. She was wearing bermuda shorts and a shirt. She gestured with her cigarette for me to sit on the couch. Then nervously, reluctantly, the fifty-three-year-old mill worker began her story in staccato statements.

"My daddy was a foreman in the mills. I've been here all my life. That's all there was. There wasn't much else. All my daddy's people were farmers, and all my mama's people were farmers. They were born in Halifax County, and they lived here all their lives. My mama and daddy were the first in the family to work in the mills.

"My daddy was my mama's overseer. I remember one time Mama went to the bathroom, and Daddy sent her home without pay for it. Another time, they had a layoff. Rather than lay off anybody else, he laid Mama off. She'd worked seventeen years in the mills, and she was mad. But he said he didn't want nobody to say he made a difference between Mama and the help. Daddy retired at the mill before Stephenson bought it, and Mama went back to the mill. She didn't even try to go back until he retired."

Did she remember 1934? That was the year of the General Textile Strike.

Virginia took a deep drag on her cigarette and answered quietly. "Yes, I remember about it. I was eleven at the time. I remember they were trying to get a union in here then. My daddy was Willie Jenkins. He worked for the mill, and he weren't for no union. See, at the time they had a picket line. They were standing at the doors not letting people go in the mills. When my daddy come up, this picket said to him, 'Bill, let me tell you something. You're not going in that mill this morning.' My daddy throwed his cigarette in front of that picket and went right in. You see, he *had* to go in to oil the machines. The union couldn't do nothin' about it."

Virginia looked across the room as though seeing a very clear picture. "I'll tell you the honest truth about what I remember about that. That was the first time I had ever seen my daddy drunk. I went to my mama, and I said, 'My daddy's dying.' She said, 'Your daddy ain't dying.' Mama was mad with him for getting drunk. She didn't think nothing was funny that day. That was the day the strike ended.

"He was drinking because he'd had it hard, and they were going back to work on Monday morning. I don't know how they decided to go back to the mills, but they were. There was a crowd outside in front of the yard, yelling out of cars, 'We won! We won! The union's won!' My daddy was on the porch. He threw down his cigarette and jumped over the banister and went up to them. 'Let me ask you something. What in the hell have you-all won? You got your house payments behind. You got your grocery bill behind. And you-all are going back to work just like you was.'" Virginia smiled. "That's my daddy for you. You see, they didn't get no union. They just struck, and then they all went back to work.

"I want to show you something. Wait here, and I'll be right back," she said on her way to the kitchen. I heard another voice, lower pitched than hers, in the rear of the house. Virginia came back with two yellowed snapshots. "This is my daddy," she said, offering me the pictures. The first was of a lean, natty man in a good suit with his fedora angled just so. A cigarette dangled from his mouth. The second was of Willie ("Bill") Jenkins laid out in his coffin. Virginia studied the photographs a moment or two. Then her mood changed.

She leaned toward me, half impish, half conspiratorial, and said, "My husband, Earl, is sitting back there off the kitchen. He worked up there for Stephenson till he lost his leg in an accident in '68. He could tell you a lot if he would. But he said he don't want to talk to no woman about no union. He doesn't even like having you in the house. But, c'mon." She winked at me. "We'll go talk to him."

Earl Davis was fifty-six, barrel-chested, and dressed in blue overalls. He sat on a straight-backed chair in a small hallway, resting his cane in front of his missing leg. The poor fellow was cornered. Now that she was at ease, Virginia was determined to have fun with us. Nothing was going to stop her. "C'mon, Earl. She's not gonna bite you."

"I know she's not gonna bite me." Then the big man blushed. He looked at me and began talking. "I can't remember much. It was just like it is now, only I was younger, and we worked longer. Twelve hours a day."

"Tell her what happened in 1934," Virginia prodded, winking at me again.

"I don't know nothing about that. I was just around."

"He didn't have nothing to do with either side," prompted Virginia.

"The union organizers were in here and like that, but I don't know nothing about it. They had something like a rally line—"

"A picket line," Virginia corrected.

"They'd be all lined up like a gang. A lot of them on strike had to give up everything they had. There was only a little work here then."

Before he had a chance to go on, Virginia changed the subject. "Tell her about the strike you were in in Tarboro when Shelby was in the second grade." She leaned against the doorjamb, fully in control of her husband and me, thoroughly enjoying herself.

"That was in '47, '48."

"I was laid off," Virginia interrupted.

"I could get a better job in Tarboro, some forty-eight miles from here. I had a cousin there," Earl explained. "They were working under a union, and the contract come up. Well, we went down in April, and they had a strike in May. My cousin walked out. There weren't but five of us left in the mill."

"Out of 280," said Virginia impatiently. "A man we'd seen before sitting on the picket lines shot in another man's house because his wife's daddy-in-law had shot the watchman. The watchman couldn't have belonged to the union anyway. He was like management."

Earl picked up the thread of his story. "There was only this handful of us that weren't union. It's not that I felt in favor of the company. It's that I couldn't have walked out." Earl stopped just short of saying he was "management." "You see, the fixer has to work the help. I was over spooling fixing and over the spoolers too. It's like with the watchman. The fixer ain't got nothing to do with it. Now, I *could* have belonged to the union, but I couldn't have walked off the job and left the machines."

"Once when we went to the picture show," Virginia cut in, "they punctured all the tires on our car with an ice pick. After we went back to work, some of them union ones told me which ones had done it. Another time, I'd gone to pick up Shelby at school. Earl was sitting on our front porch. You could see the mill from the house. I had to drive by a crowd of those union people on the road milling around. I heard the pickets say, 'Turn her over.' The next thing I knew, they were all around me. Rocking the car. About 150 of them. Then the shop steward said, 'You leave her alone, and let her go.' I wasn't even scared. I didn't have the sense to be scared. I was lucky to get out of it."

Why, if they did not feel strongly pro-company, had Earl and Virginia taken such risks when they were so far outnumbered?

"I just told you," Virginia said. "We were young and didn't have no sense. After that, the mill company had me in court all the time, speaking up for them against the strikers." She lit another cigarette, and Earl took the opportunity to pick up the conversation.

"When I came back here from Tarboro, I took a right much cut. I came back here and went into the weave room taking up quills. I worked in the River Mill. I worked up there for several years and then went on to work in the Rosemary Mill up until '68, when I had my accident and had to quit.

"These union people here say they ain't gonna strike, it ain't gonna be like it was in Tarboro."

"They ain't talking about striking," Virginia corrected. "They're *boycotting*. There ain't gonna be no fighting or fussing."

"If they do, people aren't gonna stand for that. I think it's gonna be a mess from here on in. The union ain't done nothing for the people, but the mill company ain't either. The union was in here in '65 and got voted out," Earl continued. "The only reason they got in this time was because Stephenson was working more colored, and the older ones here, they'd got out of the company. I voted against the union every time, every time. I was out for the last election, but I ain't seen nothing they done for the people. They make promises, but they can't help."

Earl was getting worked up. "In Tarboro most of the people working for the union was foreigners and Northerners. They paid them well, those union organizers. They'd go out and have steak dinners and fish dinners with their favorites. Or they get together with five or six of the young'uns. The union is gonna do for some and not for others. Now if the people could form a union of their own in here and pull together, that would be good.

"Working conditions are getting worse and worse. The mill company wants a higher production for lower cost. They're getting in one machine to do the work of four or five men. It used to be one man ran four or five machines."

As if the pent-up anger, hoarded for years in the lonely back room, had burst out, Earl went on. "That Stephenson come in here, all those big mill people. They've got plants all over. They got rid of all the local men. My wife's old boss. He went from overseer in the River Mill to weaver in the Rosemary Mill. Stephenson got him out of church one Sunday to go in to the mill. That man told them if they had to haul a man out of church, they could fire him. And they did."

Earl was becoming more agitated. "It's gonna be a strike. It's gonna be like Tarboro only worse. There'll be killings."

Virginia had been quiet too long. "Things are changing for the worse. Look at all the killings you hear about on TV all the time."

"People'd kill you just to see you die, to laugh and see you die," Earl said.

Earl and Virginia were together now, mesmerized with their own doomsday vision.

"Man's never going to be able to have peace right now," said Earl.

"Not in this world. Not according to the Bible," Virginia added. "The company's gonna keep on doing like they're doing, just like they've always done. They'll fire half the people and work the other half to death."

The Davises had worked themselves up to a pitch. Suddenly it was over. Earl sat silently nursing his memories. And Virginia said, "I was just talking to Shelby on the phone this morning, telling her I don't care whether Stephenson gives us a raise or not. If you get a raise, everything else goes up too. So what good does it do? You know, when the union election came up this time, I was surprised that people voted for it. You just don't know people, what they're for, who they're for. You don't hear nobody say nothing about it at the mill, at least not where I work at.

"But you know what does make me mad? The company is planning to get rid of the floor sweepers in my department. Then the creeler hands are gonna have to get a broom and sweep the floors three times a day. They want to give me a raise for this. I told Shelby, 'I got a job. My job is creeling warpers. My job ain't sweeping.' Now I told her, 'I weren't for no union, but this is too much.'"

Willie Jenkins' daughter stopped and pulled hard on her cigarette, then said, "I done signed me a union card." Waving away the smoke as though brushing away what she'd just revealed, Virginia added quickly, "Maybe *they* can do something about it."

Catalpa Tree
Sweet Paradise

IRENE AND KASPER SMITH

I had met Kasper Smith at the union hall too, another veteran of past labor wars. He had been on the picket line in Roanoke Rapids during the 1934 General Textile Strike. Smith was a wisp of a fellow with a small face, peaked cheeks, and round glasses. He had a mild, high-pitched voice, and, at first glance, something of the demeanor of Caspar Milquetoast. He wore a well-ironed plaid shirt, a pair of stiff blue jeans hiked way above his waist, and, snapped into one of the loops, a leather sheath with a large knife.

Kasper straddled a metal folding chair and said, "My life is so twisted up in that strike. I'd been married the year before, and my son Richard was just a baby then. At the time of that strike, I was working in Rosemary and living in the Rosemary mill village. My brother Haul was my supervisor. Only they didn't call them supervisors back then. They called them 'second hands.' Haul was a good deal older than me. See, I was only nineteen at the time of the strike.

"Now, when the strike got here, they'd already been striking up North. They were strong. But they had no business striking down South because they were weak here. We didn't have no backing. We didn't have no National Labor Relations Board then either and no labor laws. Yet we pulled a strike. We shouldn't have done it. The South hadn't even begun to organize then.

"We had a schedule for each shift of pickets. I remember it was in the fall because after I pulled my picket duty one night, me and my brother Haul went off squirrel hunting. The season had just started. We went off for a night and a day.

"The old union office used to be a dance hall, down there over the Triple R. They had an organizer named Dooley that come in here. I forget what his first name really was because some of us always called him 'Bill.' We even made up a song to 'Bill' Dooley, and we'd sing it down on the picket line."

Kasper started to sing a few bars to the tune of "Bill Bailey, Won't You Please Come Home?" He couldn't remember enough to sing a whole verse. He shook his head, a little embarrassed, and went on with what he was saying. "We were 85 per cent union here that closed those mills down. But when the strike was over, everybody hurried back to the company side. The company took a lot of us back because, see, they didn't want all the eyes all over these United States on them. Then after a little while, they began letting the strong union people go. The jobs of the union people were all in jeopardy. Mine was, even though my brother was my boss.

"I worked for about two weeks after the strike. Then they let me go. What they told me was, 'Orders is getting low. We're going to have to let you go till there's more work.' That's what griped me the most. It's sort of like it is now. They won't come right out and say you're fired because you're union. The law gets after them on that. They just kind of shift the work around so it amounts to the same thing.

"I had to move out of my house because it belonged to the company. I had my wife and baby to take care of. I couldn't begin to tell you all the people who had to leave here after that strike. After they let me go, when I was trying to get my job back, what turned my stomach was that the company wouldn't say yes and they wouldn't say no. I'd about cry and get down on my knees to them begging for a job, but they just strung you on and didn't say much of anything. I was seven or eight months out of work. I went to Danville, Burlington, and Durham looking for a job, but I couldn't find a thing.

"By that time, the union had done broke up and gone. They'd stopped distributing food like they done while the strike was on. And Dooley, the organizer, left here right after the strike. That's one reason why there's no union here today. Well, I mean, there's a union, but like back then, there's no contract. People are scared now. I think what happened in 1934 has a whole lot to do with people not being so union now."

Kasper, who was a warp tender on second shift in the River Mill, noticed it was getting close to four o'clock. "Well I'd better get going. It's time for me to go to work. Come by the house one of these days soon and meet the rest of the family and we'll talk some more."

The next week I drove out several miles west of Roanoke Rapids. Kasper's house was set back on a long meadow, the last one on his road.

A small woman with chestnut hair came to the door. Kasper's wife, Irene, wore a housedress, and she was emaciated. She brought me in to the room where Kasper was sitting on the couch with a pretty little girl and a narrow-faced woman.

Charlene, the Smiths' eleven-year-old granddaughter, whose family lived in a trailer next door, was long-limbed and hazel-eyed with shiny black hair and the fidgety energy of a child. Malara Smith Jackson, Kasper's seventy-one-year-old sister, lived in another trailer on the other side of Kasper's house. She was introduced as the family historian. As Malara and Kasper began recounting the Smith family story, Irene took a chair in a far corner of the long room, away from the couch and the sunlight of the window.

How many brothers and sisters were in the family?

Kasper straightened himself on the couch and rolled his eyes upward as though trying to remember something from long ago. "Let's see now," he said, then started in a singsong voice: "Jasper, Kasper, and Laster. Haul and Caul, Carbie, Cartha, Larkie, and Bartha. And then Lammie, Meala and Malara." Kasper smiled at his recitation, delighted with himself and the names of his siblings.

With a solemnity befitting her status as family chronicler, Malara said, "We came to Roanoke Rapids in 1920, three weeks before Christmas, when Jasper was a baby. When we came here, I got paid ten dollars and something a week, but that was because I was an experienced hand from working in the mill in Erwin, North Carolina. I liked it both places. There wasn't much difference, except we had five rooms in the mill house here, and in Erwin we only had four. I used to love spinning, but it got harder before I left the mill."

Why had the family moved to Roanoke Rapids?

"I guess because my father was a ramblin' man. We'd worked five years in Burlington. We tried farming for a year. Then we moved back to Burlington, then on to Erwin, and then here.

"I got married the year after we came to Roanoke Rapids. My husband was working in the number-three card room at the Rosemary Mill when I met him.

"I worked from 1920 to 1959 in these mills here. I lost my retirement money after I stayed out of work for five weeks. What happened was my mother had been paralyzed for two years. She had been living with me, and my older sister lived with me too to help take care of our mother while I worked. But towards the end, even with my sister right there, I took a leave of absence to help care for her.

"My husband was there then, and I sent him to have the leave paper renewed. He went down to the mill and my boss told him he'd renew it. The bossman said he didn't blame me a bit. He said if it was his mother, he'd do the same thing. So I didn't go in that Monday. The following Monday, after she died, I didn't go in either. The next Monday I did.

"Well, he'd taken me off my job I'd been working on for fifteen or twenty years. I was real hurt by that. I went to my boss about it. He said, 'Come back tomorrow and we'll see about it.' I went back the next day, and he put me on a terrible job. It was so far in the back there, nobody wanted it.

"I went back to my bossman and said to him, 'I want to know why you've got it in for me? Why do you have me way down yonder?' He said he wanted me to work that job till he could get me a better one.

"I went to the head of personnel, which was over my overseer. I told him what happened. He told me that if he was me, he'd go back and talk to my bossman. Well, I did, but he didn't talk to me the way I liked. See, he had taken up with this woman, the one he give my job to. He'd brought her over from another mill and put her on my machine.

"I told him, 'I haven't done nothing for you to have it in for me.' He told me that if I went back to that no-good machine, I could stay. I told him I wouldn't go back there. I told him, 'If that's the way you feel about it, I'd rather leave.' And that's what I did.

"I was out for a couple of years. I got me a sandwich route. I had a barbecue pit and made all kinds of sandwiches. It was hard to make a go of it. I didn't sleep night or day trying to keep it going. Finally it got too hard for me.

"I went back to see Mr. Hux, the head of personnel. He had my records out when I went in. I don't know why. He looked over my record and told me I'd always been a good worker and they'd be glad to have me back. He gave me a job again spinning.

"I worked for four more years and then had to quit because of my health. I have a real bad stomach. I've had to have surgery and everything. This time when I retired, they gave me five hundred dollars and something. They said you had to work five years before you could get retirement. They said that I lost mine when I stayed out those few years."

Kasper wanted her to backtrack. "I think she wants to know about 1934, Malara."

Malara pushed the topic away with her hands. "I can't remember about it. All I know is I was working second shift when the mills shut down. I didn't take *no* part in the union."

Kasper asked her again, and again she shunted the question. "I didn't join. I stayed out of it. Everything was closed down, except I think I remember that somebody crossed the picket line at the number-three card room at Rosemary. They had the head electrician pull the lights over there. I remember Willie Jenkins, one of the bosses, went in the mill, and some others too. They had to get the law to get them out. But that's about all I remember.

"I was out of work about three weeks. Kasper remembers the strike being longer, but that's because he was out of work longer. Not me. As soon as they opened up the mill, I was back on my job. They sent for me as soon as it was over."

Kasper nodded to his wife in the corner. "Now her daddy was big in the union back in the 1930s."

"That's right," Irene said. "My daddy was a Cherokee Indian. Dennis Lee Dover. He was a union man too. When he died, Dooley paid for his funeral."

"We've been married forty-four years, her and me," Kasper said. "She's been through a lot. I was an alcoholic, and so was she. It was pretty bad. Then I got with the A.A., and now we're both members of the Church of God."

Then he looked at me with none of the whimsy he had in naming his sisters and brothers and none of the relish with which he talked about the 1934 strike. "We're not of this world. We are not supposed to participate in anything of this world."

"Yeah, well, ain't hardly any of them in that church that *ain't* of this world," Irene said.

Kasper went on. "According to the church, you're not supposed to drink or watch TV. Now, I hardly even watch a program all the way through. Before it gets to the end, I turn away. That's how little interested I am," Kasper said, quite serious about his otherworldliness.

"My wife and me both joined the church one Sunday in March of 1974. My mother was connected with that church and so are my brothers and sisters. My church has rules: no cursing and no smoking. If you do, your name is taken off the book. And we can't belong to no organizations. We're not allowed to participate in a strike. The Bible speaks on all that. Now before anyone is read out of the church, we members vote on it."

What about all he'd just said about the 1934 strike?

Kasper seemed taken aback. "Well, they *are* real strong on no strikes. But I did that way back when. I couldn't do that now. And, well, see, I joined the union before I joined the church. I haven't joined no other organizations *since*."

Irene got up. "I'm going next door and ask my daughter-in-law if she can put my hair up for me." And Malara Jackson decided she had to go too.

"Let's go outside," Charlene suggested to her grandfather. We walked down the hill from the house that Kasper had built himself. Kasper took steady strides across his land. Charlene, barefooted, ran lightly beside him. As we approached Kasper's seven hives, the bees started to swarm. "Better circle on out. Don't get too close or they'll come after you," Kasper warned. We walked back up the incline, around to Kasper's half-acre garden and his apple and pear orchard.

"Want to see my pet pig?" Charlene asked and led us down the far side of the garden, by the fence running along a small pond. All the way down she clapped her hands and called, "Arnold! Arnold!" She got the name from "Green Acres," one of her favorite television programs. Hearing Charlene's voice, an energetic, red-haired pig waddled to the edge of the sty, clearly delighted to see her mistress. Arnold put her snout through the fencing. Metal prongs were in her nostrils. "My grandfather put those in so she couldn't root." Charlene stuck her arm through the fencing and stroked the pig. Arnold shuffled her feet and jiggled her bulk. She looked supremely content being near Charlene.

Charlene not only had a pig; she also had a cageful of pet white mice, all of them called Rat. She got them at Rose's, the chain-store five and dime. She had a dog named Galin and a snake dog named Snoopy. Sweet childhood paradise.

As we walked past the pond, Kasper pointed to a slender-trunked tree with wide, heart-shaped leaves. "That's a catalpa tree. I've got it in case I want to fish. Don't have to go for bait. Just go and get my rod, and I'm all set."

I had no idea what he meant. Charlene stood with one bare foot resting on the other, as her grandfather explained that big, fat fishing worms gathered on the leaves, plump for the picking. "When you want to fish, you just pull them off. You can sell them too if you want."

As we looked at the tree, we saw Irene in fat, pink curlers leaving her daughter-in-law's trailer, going back to her own house. Kasper walked rapidly now. Time was getting short before he had to leave for the mill. Charlene was still going at her own child's pace, dreamy slow and darting fast.

"Want to see the puppies?" Charlene asked.

"I guess there's time to look at them," Kasper said, heading toward his pointers.

Charlene ran to the female and three young pups. "That's the papa over there," she said, nodding toward the adjacent pen.

Kasper had chickens behind his house, and he couldn't resist showing them off as well. New Hampshire Reds were in one hennery and pullets in another. In a cage beyond them, isolated, was a game cock.

"Have you ever seen a chicken fight?" Kasper asked. I told him I hadn't. He took the cock from its cage and put it in the coop with a rooster and the hens. The hens scurried to the far corner of the enclosure.

The two fighters stood off. Their feathers ruffled. They both jumped high. Attacked. Sprung in the air. Attacked again. Danced around, neither ever taking its eyes off the other.

"If they had their spurs on now, one of them'd be dead," Kasper said.

The two males climbed into the hen house, which the females had vacated, and they danced again. There was no room for high leaps. They came out, squared off and, almost too quick to see, the cock lunged at the rooster. This time, the rooster climbed into the hen house alone, defeated. The cock strutted around the coop and crowed. The fight was over.

Charlene and I went inside the house. Kasper got his cap and dinner pail. His mind had already left his land.

"They won't let us, the boys on the warp crew, even get our own rags now. They've started locking them up in the office and making us ask for them. We want to know why they are giving us such a hard time." Kasper smiled. "I'll tell you why. Because the warp crew are strong union. Clyde Bush down at the union hall told me if all the members were like the warp crew, we'd have the strongest union around."

Kasper said good-bye to Irene, who was seated again in the recliner chair in the dark corner, and hugged Charlene. Just as he was going out the door, he turned to me. "Now my wife's got some things she can tell you. She's worked all her life in the mills, and she knows a lot."

He went out into the hot afternoon to work. He would not be back until after midnight to the still and quiet of the land.

As Irene, the diminutive figure who up until now had said so little, began to talk, her granddaughter stretched out on the couch. The chair Irene was sitting in and her dress were muted.

Even her pink curlers were not vivid in this shadowy light. She was somber, inconspicuous. Her voice, small and indistinct.

"I've worked all my life in those mills, and I have cancer. I need therapy, but I can't get it because I can't draw a dime of disability. I was born in Anderson, South Carolina, on July 22, 1916. That's a big cotton-mill town too. J. P. Stevens owns it now too, but it didn't own it back then.

"I was the oldest of six children. I don't know where my mother was from, but my father was from Gaffney, South Carolina, about 150 miles from Anderson. My mother's maiden name was Ethel Smith. What I remember most clearly in my life is the day she died. I'm sixty-one years old, and it's just as fresh in my mind today as I'm looking at you.

"She was pregnant, but, of course, being seven years old, I didn't notice. She told me to take my little sister, who was four, up the street to her sister's. My mama was going to make us cornbread and buttermilk for our supper, and she said she wanted to borrow some buttermilk.

"She was in labor at that time. I know that now. We lived in the mill village. Next door there were mill girls playing in their yard. Their mother had jumped into one of them wells and drowned herself the day before. So we stopped and talked with them. They were our playmates. Then we went on to my aunt's, and then we went on home.

"When we got there, the yard was full of cars. Well, you know, back in 1924, there weren't many cars. My daddy came out on the porch and told us to go to a neighbor's house until he called us. He came for us after a while. He took me by the hand and picked up my little sister. He brought us into our mother's room. He didn't stop at her bed. No, he didn't stop there. He walked over to the trunk on the far side of the room and pulled back the cover on top of it. That little baby was lying there. He said to us, 'This is your sister, and she's dead.'

"Now you know, a seven-year-old child ain't going to know too much about dying. My daddy said to me, 'Irene, your mama's dying, and she wants to talk to you.' I had a beauty of a mother. She took my hand. 'Irene, I'm going to leave you, and I'm going to leave you in charge of the younger ones. Always mind the one you're having to live with.' She was singing 'God Be with You Till We Meet Again,' and then she was saying, 'Our Father, who art in heaven.' Those were the last words I ever heard her say.

"I don't know if they embalmed back then or not, but they came and got her and brought her on her way, you know. They buried her the next day. She was only twenty-four. She had the baby in her arms. The day they buried her, one of my aunts stayed with us until about bedtime. It was February, and we had three fireplaces in the house going, and the wood stoves going too. There was nobody in the house but us three children, me and my sister, Hazel, and my little brother, Jack.

"I figured my daddy had gone back to work, and he'd be home soon. There was no more coal. I put some wood in the stove and closed the damper so it would hold the fire all night. In the morning, I cooked whatever there was to eat, and after a while there weren't no more wood. We walked the three or four blocks to my aunt's. I told her our wood had burned up and we didn't have no coal neither.

"Well, she took us and kept us until dinner time, twelve o'clock. Fed us and carried us back home to wait for my father. But he didn't come. Anyhow, to make a long story short, we didn't see him no more.

"My aunt kept my little brother and give me to one of the cousins. She had a neighbor take my sister. But, see, that's one thing mama said before she died: Don't separate us. So my aunt got my sister and me in an orphanage in Toccoa, Georgia. My brother was in a boys' home six miles away. We had to pick cotton with the boys over at their home. The people who ran the orphanage were Holiness people.

"We children never had enough to eat. We were always hungry. On Fridays we'd get one slice of loaf bread and one glass of water. That was their religion. They called it fasting. On Sundays we children would sneak down to the kitchen and get into the pot of navy beans they left sitting on the stove. See, they did all their cooking on Saturday and nothing on Sunday. That was part of their religion too. We'd always put more water on the beans to raise the level up so they wouldn't miss the beans. We never got caught.

"Well, we was poor. We was about fifty girls. We'd get so cold we'd pull the mattresses off the beds and pile them one on top of the other and crawl in between to try to stay warm. There was no heat at all.

"We had lice. They had to cut our hair off. And we had the itch. That's a skin disease that gets between your fingers and toes. They'd take a number-three washtub and fill it with lard and sulphur and some other kind of medicine. Maybe turpentine. We'd line up. They had long sticks with something on the end. They'd dip into this stuff and swab us down good. And we'd cry and cry.

"All of us looked so bad. We weren't allowed to come out when inspectors or visitors come round. They'd take us children and put us under that church in an enclosed porchlike thing. They'd hide us under there. Sometimes as high as fifteen or twenty of us would be under there. See, the money was coming in, but they used it for themselves and for their families. Well, we stayed there a year. I wasn't but eight years old."

Charlene was sitting bone straight now, listening to her grandmother. She looked stricken. Irene had never told the storybook child her nightmare tales.

"Well, you know news traveled slow in 1925, but it finally got to my aunt, my mother's sister who was a missionary in China. I was named for her. The Essie part. The Irene part is for a mill in Gaffney. See, my whole name when I was born was Essie Irene Dover.

"Well, my mother's sister had worked her way through college. She'd gone to school in Greenwood, South Carolina. When she heard what had happened to us, she sent word back for us to be put in a home in Greenwood that she knew was good.

"So my aunt who was looking out for us, the one that put us in that home in Georgia, carried us to Greenwood, to a Baptist orphanage. Me and my sister. She took my brother and kept him. In the meantime, I hadn't seen my daddy since the funeral.

"There were 450 of us children on acres and acres of land. There were big brick houses and twenty-seven girls to a house. We went to school from eight until twelve in the morning and from seven until at nine at night. And we each had a chore to do in the dormitories. We were divided into three sizes: small, medium, and grown. The youngest was about three. You were graded on your chore just like in school. Like when we'd do the kitchen floor, each of us had certain blocks of tile to scrub.

"Once I got out of there to go to Clinton, South Carolina. See, there was a women's circle there. They'd send me four boxes of clothes a year—summer, spring, winter, and fall. They sent them according to my measurements and everything. This one time, they sent me train fare to come to Clinton, so that the women who supplied my clothes could see me, you know. They met me at the train station, this lady and her daddy. We stopped in front of a long jailhouse. The bars were three stories high. See, her daddy looked after the prison. This lady was the head of the group that had sent my clothes. We got out and went in, and we sang in their little church. That night you could hear the prettiest music you could ever have in a prison. They got me to sing at church the next day. That was so all the ones who sent me the clothes could see me.

"When it was time to go, they sent me off with a great big basket of fruit. It was so heavy I couldn't tote it. The conductor had to help me. I was so happy. I thought I'd have all the friends in the world with that big basket of fruit. But when I got back, the lady who ran the home took it into the kitchen and made a fruit salad out of it.

"I understand now. She did the right thing. But at the time I thought me and my sister and three or four friends could share it. I cried and cried about it because I guess I was on the stingy side. Well, anyway, that's the end of that story."

Irene looked smaller than her granddaughter, this frail woman with the big pink curlers. Her childhood had one more chapter. She related it in an even, beyond-emotion voice.

"One day when I'd been there at that home about five years, me and my girl friend, Pauline, were walking by the office the big bosses worked in. This taxicab passed us, and I said to Pauline, 'Maybe those men will give us a nickel.' We took off running. One man got out. The other one stayed in and went on with the cab. The first man started up the steps, and me and Pauline started up with him.

"I told my friend, 'My daddy looks like that man.' The man on the steps turned and said to me, 'You ain't Irene?' I said, 'Yeah'—

I mean, I said, 'Yes, sir.' Well, he grabbed me up and started lov-
ing me, you know. Finally he put me down, and I run back to tell
my sister. You know how young'uns are in places like that.

"I told her, 'Our daddy's come!' She started to cry. 'It's not our
daddy. It's someone coming to kidnap us and kill us.' I said, 'No.
No, he ain't. He's our daddy.' So after a while, he come on down
to the dormitory. He asked if we wanted to go home. I said yes.
See, I didn't have no better sense than that. I had just turned
fourteen, and I was old enough to go and work in the mill.

"We had to get permission from my aunt in China to go. In
about two or three weeks, the letter came. My sister and me took
the train to Roanoke Rapids. We slept in a berth. We had breakfast on the train. So that's how my sister and me come out of that
home. And we've had hell ever since.

"My daddy was about forty at the time, and he had married
someone six years older than me. She was jealous. They had two
children under three. One of them had died, and the other one
was afflicted when it was born. It never did walk. It slid on its tail
and pulled its poor leg behind it.

"Daddy made me quit school. I was in the fifth grade. I cried
and cut up so bad he let me go back for a while. But then my
stepmother went back to work, and she needed somebody to keep
house. So, halfway through the year, my daddy made me quit
school for good and stay home. Me and my husband got married
when I was sixteen. I got married to get away. I worked in the
mills all my life. Life just got worse and worse from there. It's
been hell."

Before the week was out, Irene Smith's hell was over. This
woman named after a mill had died of cancer.

The Sound of Protest,
the Rattle of Looms

MAURINE HEDGEPETH

Maurine Mayton Hedgepeth's birth was dramatic. On February 22, 1932, a mob bent on a lynching had gathered outside the Patterson Mill Store between the Rosemary and Patterson mills. A six-year-old girl had been raped and killed the day before. Upstairs above the store the murderer was on trial in a special session of the municipal court, across the hall from the apartment where Alice Mayton was in labor. The mill company doctor who had come to deliver the baby had to fight his way through the unruly crowd that was determined to get its hands on the murderer before the police could spirit him out of town to safety.

Maurine, the child brought into the world that day, amid protest and the rattle of looms, grew up to spend her life with the sounds that accompanied her birth.

By coincidence, the day she was born was the bicentennial of the birth of another Southerner, the first President of the United States. This child, brought forth at the hand of a company doctor in a company-owned apartment in a company store building in a company town, grew up to fight for American ideals as unpopular in her time and place as democracy was in Washington's. Principles such as the right of workers to organize, the right to free assembly, freedom of choice.

"I've got a real purpose for being here, and I'm *glad* I'm here,"

Maurine said years later, when her actions had affected the mills that were the lifeblood of her town. "I believe that everybody is here on earth for a purpose, and I believe I know what my purpose is. I think it is to do the best I can with the little knowledge that God gave me. I think I can make this a better place. I really do.

"For a long time, I didn't know. I thought I was here for somebody to pick on. I mean, I knew there was a reason for me being here, but now it's totally different. One day about twenty years ago I woke up and I knew that things had changed, that there was a purpose for me other than just being somebody to clean up the table after everyone had eaten.

"Working at the mill may have been the start of the change. A long time ago, when I went and saw what my father was going through at the plant, I knew I wanted to do *something* about it, but I didn't know what.

"To begin with, I was only involved with the mills through my father. The mill really had nothing to do with me, other than whatever hurt him hurt me. But then, when I worked in the plant myself, and I saw that conditions were even worse than I imagined them to be—well. . . . There is a reason for me to have to have suffered through the things that I have, and I think it makes me a better person. Let's get off this."

Maurine was embarrassed by the personal talk. She was in a duster, barefoot, forty-five years old, sitting in her dim living room, thinking about her life and the choices she has made and the price she has paid and is paying for them.

When Maurine was a child, she did not identify strongly with the mills. It was not until she was a grown woman that she realized that improving conditions in the mills was her own battle. Partly this was because the Mayton family was unusual in Roanoke Rapids. They never lived in a mill village. The only time they lived in a company-owned building was when their daughter Maurine was born. They were not dependent on the mill company for their livelihood, for every month Maurine's father, LeRoy, received a pension check from the U. S. Navy. Because Alice Mayton and her children were Catholic, the Maytons lived outside the mainstream of southern Protestantism. The Maytons had had experiences broader than those usually available to North

Louis Harrell, victim of brown lung, five days before dying.

Lucy Taylor, the first president of the Roanoke Rapids chapter of the Carolina Brown Lung Association.

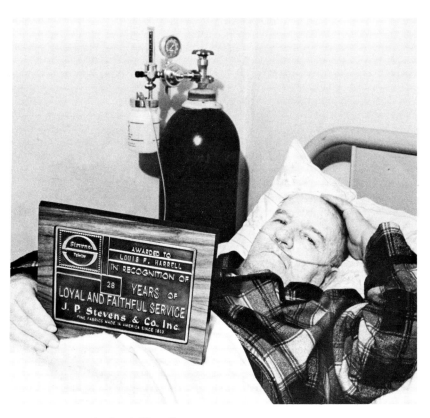

Retirement for Louis Harrell.

A fallen brother of the Carolina Brown Lung Association.

LOUIS FONTAINE HARRELL
1915 — 1978

Brown Lung Association
COTTON DUST KILLS

Louis Harrell's widow, Lillian, and family.

Carolina Brown Lung Association.

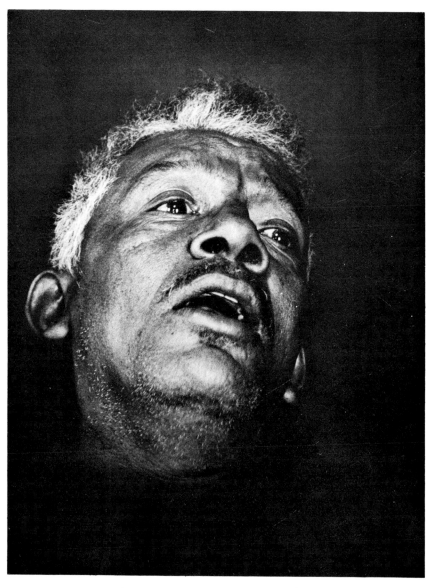

J. P. Stevens worker in Roanoke Rapids, one of 35,000 U.S. textile workers with brown lung disease.

Carolina mill-working families. Both Alice and LeRoy Mayton had lived full lives before they ever worked a day in a cotton mill.

Maurine's mother, Alice Mary Pelkey, a French-Canadian, was one of the thirteen children of Julia Pelkey and her husband, George, a cabinet- and fiddle-maker. When Alice was thirteen, she traveled to Portland, Maine, rented bed space in a boarding house for women, and began working as a dietitian in the State Street Hospital.

Maurine's father, LeRoy Mayton, was a North Carolinian who spent his childhood traveling from mill town to mill town with his five younger brothers, his mother, Robina Frances, and his father, John Thomas Mayton. LeRoy's father installed winding machines and taught workers how to operate them. For a while, the Mayton family had lived in Roanoke Rapids, where John Thomas installed winders in the New Mill.

Alice Pelkey and LeRoy Mayton had met when she was thirteen and he was twenty-two and in the Navy. His ship had hosted an open house in Portland. When Alice Pelkey crossed the gangplank, she caught the eye of the bantamweight American sailor. She spoke little English, and he knew only a catch phrase or two in French, but before his ship left port, Alice Pelkey and LeRoy Mayton were engaged.

Six months after LeRoy had sailed, a parcel arrived for Alice from China: a quarter-carat diamond ring to confirm the betrothal. Alice asked a friend named Betty, a nurse in the hospital, to write LeRoy a letter in English. When his response came in the mail, Betty translated it to Alice. The courtship by mail continued for thirteen years, as LeRoy lived adventures that would fuel his memories in his later years.

He sailed on the *Kearsarge*, a wooden ship. He was out on the high seas, he liked to tell his own daughter years later, in the days when ships were wood and men were steel. LeRoy Mayton survived World War I, as a Chinese fortuneteller had predicted; when his ship was attacked and sunk, he was one of four survivors.

LeRoy's adventuring took him right up to his retirement at age thirty-five. In 1927, when he was discharged from the Navy at Norfolk, Virginia, he felt it was time to settle down. He wanted a small, quiet place to raise a family. He traveled to Roanoke

Rapids, where three of his brothers were working in the mills, and got a job in the cloth room at the New Mill.

LeRoy had not forgotten his French fiancée, who by this time was twenty-six. He sent money to Alice to take the train to North Carolina. The couple married, and Alice got a job as a winder in the River Mill, working on a machine like the ones her father-in-law had installed years before. LeRoy became working boss in charge of his noon-to-midnight shift. He brought home seven dollars a week.

Before they came to Roanoke Rapids, Alice and LeRoy Mayton had been exposed to something few people in town in the early 1930s had experienced: unions. When the first textile organizer came to Roanoke Rapids in 1934, the year of the General Textile Strike, Alice and LeRoy invited him into their home. The organizer, Jay Dooley, lived with the Maytons when Maurine was two years old.

One of the houses Maurine was raised in with her three brothers and one sister was a brick house on Roanoke Avenue. She could see the Rosemary Mill from the house and the company store where she had been born.

When Maurine was growing up, her mother regularly rode the bus to the New Mill, where she had been transferred. When the handsome young bus driver, Julian MacDonald Hedgepeth, known universally as "Doodle," was driving, Alice never had to walk to the bus stop; she was his favorite, and he picked her up in front of the house.

They had a routine they repeated daily. As soon as Alice paid her ten cents and had taken the seat directly behind the driver, Doodle started.

"I'm gonna marry your daughter, Mrs. Mayton. I'm gonna marry Maurine."

"No you ain't. No you ain't." By this time, the volatile Gallic woman had developed a southern accent as thick as buttermilk.

Alice was half-kidding and half-serious. Doodle meant it.

When Julian Hedgepeth was six years old, he caught doodle-bugs. "Doodle-catching" was a childhood game in the rural North Carolina of those days, when money for toys was scarce. A doodlebug is an ant lion. In its larval stage, it digs a hole in loamy soil about a half inch wide and a quarter inch deep. The insect lives at the bottom of the hole, waiting for an ant or other small insect to tumble in. Then it quickly snatches the prey with powerful jaws and sucks it dry.

Sometimes children had doodle-catching contests, the prize being temporal glory to the one bagging the most ant lions. The game, properly played, involved stirring in the hole with a straw and at the same time chanting:

> *"Doodle, doodle, come out!*
> *Your house is on fire!"*

Supposedly the words caused the doodlebug to scuttle out backwards from the hole in a great hurry.

Julian Hedgepeth had his own method for catching doodlebugs. He used a wild onion for bait. He dangled the onion in the hole until the doodlebug made a grab for it. Then he pulled out the insect and added it to his collection. He wasn't catching the doodles for a contest; he used them for bait to fish on the Roanoke River.

Julian spent so much time catching doodlebugs in his front yard that when neighbors wanted him to run an errand, they would call out, "Doctor Doodlebug! Doctor Doodlebug!"

The little boy knew what that meant. Someone needed Dr. J. W. Martin. He dropped his wild onion, left his cache, and ran to the doctor's. When he got to the Martin house, young Hedgepeth knocked at the door, and the Patterson Mill's doctor dropped the car keys into the little boy's hand. "Doctor Doodlebug" hurried to the garage to warm up the automobile, and Dr. Martin dropped his helper back home before going on to his patient. Doodle slammed the car door and picked up his wild onion where he had left off.

Everyone in Patterson Village, from Weaver Creek all the way back to the high school on Hamilton Street, knew Doctor Doodlebug. The mill village gave him his name and his first job.

Doodle's first paying job—he had never taken money for fetching the doctor—was a nickel a week hauling home the family groceries in his wagon. Doodle and his father went together on payday, and Andrew picked out $5.40 worth of supplies for the family.

When he got a little older, Doodle helped his father with the garden and chickens in the back yard. And as a boy, he watched his father make home brew in the woodshed. Later, Doodle and his brothers, Linwood and Buddy, helped Andrew work on the family's 1927 four-door Buick. Once, when Linwood was at the wheel, the car took off, smashed through Andrew Hedgepeth's home-brew bottles, rammed through the woodshed and on into the coal shed. Mostly though, the car just sat. During the 1934 General Textile Strike, the car was parked under a shade tree near the Patterson Mill. When Doodle carried supper down to his father on the picket line, Andrew Hedgepeth and his friends had the car seats out and were playing cards and singing, "You'll never make a living 'round a cotton mill" and "The poor get poorer and the rich get richer."

Before they went to work in the mill, Andrew and Minnie Hedgepeth had been farming people in Halifax County, like their parents before them. The couple had moved to the Patterson Mill Village in 1926, the day their son Julian MacDonald was born.

The Hedgepeth family—Andrew and Minnie, Andrew's mother, the three sons, and a daughter named Naomi—lived in a three-room house on Williams Street that they rented from the mill for $1.20 a week.

The Patterson Mill Village was Doodle's childhood world, and it was richly peopled. Mr. Hawkins, the ice man, came around every day with his horse and wagon selling chunks of ice for from five to fifty cents. The Hedgepeths almost always got fifteen cents' worth. And Mr. Melvin sold penny candy and vegetables from his mule wagon. On Fridays, when he sold mackerel and perch, women waited with fish pans.

Doodle recalls the black man who emptied the contents of the privies behind the mill houses. George Clintshaw was employed by the Patterson Mill and worked a regular daily shift. He lived in the "colored village" within the Patterson Mill Village. Until it was razed in 1977, the "colored village" was on Marshall Street, around the corner from where Doodle and Maurine live today.

Doodle remembers Clintshaw in his Sunday best, for he was also a preacher. On Sunday mornings he came out on his front porch, where a piano was set up. People from all over the Patterson Mill Village, mostly children, black and white, and many of their parents, including Andrew and Minnie Hedgepeth, gathered in the Clintshaw front yard and sang and prayed with Brother George.

The Hedgepeth family had a hard time making ends meet. Just before payday, the family dieted on fatback, carob syrup, and homemade biscuits. On occasional Sundays the Hedgepeths fried a chicken and indulged in a banana pudding. During the week, Doodle did not eat in the morning or at school. When he came home in the afternoon, he helped himself to two biscuits and swallowed a half can of Carnation milk. Minnie Hedgepeth had to leave for her shift at the mill by three, but before she left she fixed supper for the family.

Andrew Hedgepeth, not able to make an adequate living, left the mill for a job on the police force. Later he took a job as a prison guard at the Caledonia State Prison Farm. Four years after he left the mill, Andrew died of a stroke at age fifty-five.

After his father's death, Doodle helped support the family. When he was fourteen, he got a job working for Carl Murray's Bus Line. He gassed up the buses and fixed tires. When he was sixteen, he got his driver's license, a year under the legal age. Then he started driving the bus. His route was uptown on the Avenue, and he enjoyed "hauling people around," especially Alice Mayton. He was as conscientious on this job as he had been when he was just a tad of a "Doctor Doodlebug." Doodle ranged all over town, from the river to the railroad depot. But his world, his home, would always be the Patterson Mill Village.

Maurine was a stranger to mill-village life until she married Doodle, when he was nineteen and she was the eighth-grade beauty queen. The year after Maurine's marriage, the union came back to Roanoke Rapids for the first time since the 1934 strike. Workers in the Patterson Mill had called for a representation election. Two unions answered the appeal: the Textile Workers Union of America, then part of the Congress of Industrial Organizations, and District 50 of John L. Lewis's United Mine Workers Union.

On December 4, 1946, 344 voted for union representation and 328 voted against it. Because the union vote was split—192 voting for the UMW and 152 for the TWUA—Patterson Mill workers did not win any representation.

In the early part of their marriage, neither Maurine nor Doodle worked in the mills. On her summer vacation from high school, Maurine worked as a waitress at the Croatan Cafe, next door to WCBT. At the radio station, Jesse Helms, then an announcer, had a standing order for coffee and juice. Nearly every morning when Maurine brought over his breakfast, Helms would tell his listening audience that a pretty young girl had just come in. Years later Maurine said, "Now I wish I had poured coffee over him because of how he's fought the labor laws." In 1978 Helms led the filibuster on the Senate floor that defeated the labor law reform bill.

One Sunday night in 1948, when Maurine was sixteen, she went to her first union meeting. Workers in the River Mill had also called for union representation, and the TWUA had sent in an organizer, Toby Mendes. Maurine accompanied her parents to the textile-union hall, where Alice and LeRoy Mayton had gone so many times before during the 1934 textile strike. Maurine said, "I went to be with my parents, to get informed and to see what was going on."

On March 12, 1948, the TWUA won its first election in Roanoke Rapids when the River Mill, built by Major Emry, voted for union representation. On May 10 the Roanoke Mills Company, then part of Simmons, met with the union for the first time in contract negotiations. The mill was represented in the meeting by its top officials, including its president, Frank Williams.

On August 6, 1948, another union representation election was held at the Patterson Mill. In this election 192 voted for the TWUA and 212 voted for no union. Twenty votes were challenged and four votes were voided. The union had suffered a serious setback.

On October 16, in a letter to TWUA headquarters in New York, Lewis Conn, the North Carolina state director for the union, wrote, "Herewith are my impressions and suggestions concerning Roanoke Rapids. The people are understandably demoralized. A serious error was made in not setting up immediately after the election a steward structure, along with certain other trappings of a functioning local organization.

"I do not believe that we have the people. We are going to have to win them all over again through performance and activity. Either that or lose the situation in the long run. We've got to have something concrete around which to build an organization and develop a little militancy.

"In the upcoming negotiation meeting with the company," Conn continued, "we will seek to maneuver Williams into a verbal agreement to put the grievance clause into operation at once insofar as it is agreed on, including arbitration to the extent that it is agreed. Also to apply at once whatever else is agreed on—such as seniority and bulletin boards. If this can be done, we can really build a functioning organization which may develop enough solidarity to win out on the other key issues in the coming months. We would hope to reach the point where one day we can tell Williams, 'We want a contract by such and such a time—or else.'

"Whether we succeed in this maneuver or not, a high-powered administrative job is essential right now if we are to get the workers organized. Win or lose, the union must make issues out of layoffs, out of seniority, which are weakening the union, and every other type of grievance."

The union position in Roanoke Rapids worsened as 1948 wore on. In his December 14 report to Emil Rieve, the general president of the Textile Workers Union of America, Lewis Conn wrote about the deteriorating situation: "The company is virtually refusing to bargain. Bargaining with this company has boiled down to the key issues. The company knows that the workers lack militancy and cohesion and is virtually refusing to bargain, insofar as the remaining issues are concerned."

Turning to the matter of union organization, Conn reported, "At long last an organization has been set up of stewards and general committee. This should have been done following certification. A few grievances have been taken up; many more which should have been raised (and on some of which I was confident of a settlement) were not taken up.

"I am convinced that the only possible hope for saving this situation is to *organize* the workers and to build militancy through processing grievances and complaints. We do not yet have a union there, merely a top negotiating committee."

Conn described the company's tactics, which were almost exactly the same as those used by Stevens thirty years later. The grievance procedure was undercut because there were no arbitration rights, which gave the company the final say. As would happen in contract negotiations in the 1970s, the mill management obstinately refused any type of checkoff. As for arbitration of work loads, Conn wrote, "The company offers the right to strike in lieu thereof—after telling us they plan drastic changes, and that they are offering the right to strike because they can replace economic strikers under Taft-Hartley. The company appears unbending on every one of these issues."

On April 13, 1949, a decertification election was held at the River Mill. The workers voted on whether they wanted to continue union representation or not. They decided against the union.

On March 23, just before the vote, Lewis Conn had reported back to union headquarters. "A surprise move for decertification was launched last week. There are sufficient signatures to file, some of them by our own people, who signed either out of fear or as a challenge to the company. We decided against blocking the election despite the fact that we had enough information to do it, and expect an early election—perhaps by April 15. Since the contract was virtually completed, except for the checkoff, we have a basis from which to wage a campaign, now under way. In many ways, I welcome the election. If we win it, we are in solid. If we lose, we'll leave a bad situation clean, and thus be able to return."

Returning was not so easy. The union, soundly routed from Roanoke Rapids, left in its wake many jobless union supporters who had been fired after the union lost. The risks involved in being a union supporter struck Maurine. People she had known a long time, family friends and neighbors, were fired. Seeing the union pack up after the defeat left Maurine with a profound wariness of unions and union organizers.

When Maurine was in the twelfth grade, she became pregnant. Rowland Hedgepeth, called "Nook," was born on Christmas Day 1950, when Maurine was eighteen years old. The birth of this child meant her giving up high school.

As he grew older, Nook developed asthma. At the time, Doodle was working second shift as a loom fixer at the New Mill. He brought home thirty-five dollars a week. Although mill workers contributed fifty cents a week for medical care at the company-supported hospital, the doctor sent the Hedgepeth baby to the Duke University Medical Center in Durham. The local hospital was not equipped for the extensive allergy tests and treatment the child needed. The mill did not pay any of the Duke doctor bills, which took two of Doodle's paychecks a month.

Maurine and Doodle's second son, William, was born March 26, 1955. When he was three months old and Nook was five, the couple made a decision: Maurine would go to work long enough to pay off the medical bills and get the family in the black. She got a job at the New Mill as a magazine filler.

Maurine was able to get on the third shift, so she could work while the children slept. In her twenty-three years, she had never before been in a weave room. After her first night's work she was utterly exhausted, overcome by the dust flying everywhere, the noise, the humidity, the speed of the looms, the insufferable heat. She returned home shortly after seven in the morning, and her day as a mother began.

In the mid-1950s mill work in Roanoke Rapids was not as regimented as it later became. Maurine's job was keeping her looms filled with the magazines which held the bobbins. The weaver she worked for taught her how to weave so that Maurine could relieve her. "She taught me, and I'd weave and run my job too so she could sit back and breathe for a while. Then she'd do the same thing for me."

Not long after Maurine went to work, J. P. Stevens bought the plants. Maurine knew nothing about Stevens, but she had heard rumors running through the weave room that the mills were being bought by another company.

"I needed a job, and I had a job. It didn't matter to me who owned the mills so long as somebody was keeping them in operation. If I could have known then what I know now, it would have been a very bad day for me. The Simmons Company was a whole lot better to work for."

Within a year of its takeover, Stevens moved all the looms from the New Mill weave room, where Maurine worked, to the Rosemary Mill. The change did not affect her. In fact, the coming

of J. P. Stevens to Roanoke Rapids brought Maurine her first promotion. One day, when she had all her magazines filled, she was
sitting on the windowsill, dreamily looking out on the Avenue
where the house she lived in as a girl had stood and where Doodle
had courted her. She remembered sitting on the porch looking at
the mill she now worked in.

She had a quill, an empty bobbin, in her hand and was absent-
mindedly hitting it on the back of the loom. Suddenly she realized she had broken out half the warp. She quickly started tying
in the ends just as her overseer walked by and saw the mess she
had made.

He asked her what had happened, and she told him. To her
surprise, what he was interested in was her repair work. It showed
him that she knew how to weave. He asked if she had been
through a training program. She told him no, that the weaver she
worked with had taught her.

"Well, I think I'll give you a job. You've done a good repair job
here."

He gave her a piece job running four looms and filling her own
magazines. After a production engineer came to check efficiency
in the weave room, Maurine was given six looms and no longer
had to fill magazines. Delighted, she brought home her increased
paycheck.

Some, including Maurine's father, did not have such pleasant
experiences with the new management. In 1956, when LeRoy was
sixty-four years old, Stevens took him off his job as a cloth inspector and put him to work lifting rolls of cloth weighing from 100
to 250 pounds.

"I used to go and see him pick up those rolls of cloth," Maurine
said. "He was an old man. I just hated Stevens for doing people
that way. Daddy would come home at night, and I'd hear him
say, 'I'll see them in hell before I quit.'"

Mayton would have lost his retirement benefits had he quit before he was sixty-five. He stuck it out and, after twenty-seven
years' service, got $42.10 a month from the mill.

When Maurine had gone to work in the mill, she had one goal
—earning money for her young family. She was not about to risk
her wages. Seeing her father tote heavy bolts of cloth acted as a
catalyst: It made her angry.

Her first act to improve conditions in the mill was seemingly small. When she first started working, a couch and chair had been provided in the restroom. Later these were replaced by a wooden bench. When J. P. Stevens removed the bench, Maurine and the other women in her weave room protested.

"We told them all it would cost us to get that bench back was the price of a stamp. We told them we were going to write to the Labor Board. They didn't talk to us for six weeks. We kept it up, and we got our bench back."

In the next few years, many Roanoke Rapids workers were angry because Stevens had replaced local mill workers with South Carolinians, increased work loads, and made arbitrary changes in job descriptions.

The loom fixers were particularly dissatisfied. Under Stevens' management, they were required to do maintenance work that they had never done before. Under the leadership of a worker named William Johnson, a Loom Fixers Club was formed. After the club—a union of sorts—walked off the job, the men succeeded in forcing Stevens to meet some of their demands.

In the autumn of 1958 the doffers in four Roanoke Rapids mills also staged a walkout. More and more workers were disgruntled. Several wrote letters to the southern regional headquarters of the TWUA in Charlotte, North Carolina, asking that an organizer be sent to help them win a union election.

In September 1958 a new organizing drive began. The union hall used in 1934 and 1948 had long since been condemned for gatherings by the fire department because the floors of the old building had weakened. The TWUA tried to reserve time for a meeting in one of the city-owned recreation centers. The request was denied on the grounds that the union was a private organization, despite the fact that an array of business-oriented fraternal organizations held meetings regularly in the centers. The paper mill in Roanoke Rapids was already unionized, and the paperworkers union offered their union hall for a meeting; 450 textile workers showed up.

About this time, William Johnson approached Maurine Hedgepeth to ask her to sign a union blue card.

"I wouldn't do it. First, there are a lot of people I don't trust, and he was one of them. And second, if I am going to sign a

union blue card, I'd put it in an envelope and mail it to the
Charlotte union office. That way I *know* that nobody has access
to it except the union. Then I don't have to worry about somebody getting mad at me and showing it to the company.

"I believe in unions because my mother and father were out on
strike in 1934 and signed up again in 1948, but I still wouldn't get
involved. I was afraid I would lose my job. I wouldn't even go to a
meeting in 1958. They didn't really need *me*. All they needed was
my vote, and they got it. That's the way I felt about it then.
Remember, there was that strike going on in Henderson at the
time, and I hadn't forgotten 1948, when so many people lost their
jobs and were walking the streets. So I just waited, and we lost
that election."

The union was soundly trounced in the May 1, 1959, election:
885 voted for the TWUA, and 1,664 voted against it. The problems that existed before the union defeat were left unsolved, and
workers continued writing the Charlotte union office. In 1963 the
union again sent an organizer to Roanoke Rapids.

Maurine's attitude about publicly identifying herself with the
union had not changed. As she had done before, she filled out a
union blue card and sent it to the Charlotte office. She did not
offer to help the man the union had sent. "Over the years, I had
gotten to a place where I didn't trust the men organizers because
of them holding elections and then leaving."

Then the union sent another organizer to Roanoke Rapids, Virginia Keyser. Maurine said to herself, "Hm, things are going to be
different this time."

The woman organizer came to the Hedgepeth house. She asked
Maurine to be one of the union committees.

Maurine told her no. "I wish you all the luck in the world, but
there's no way."

Virginia told her, "Well, without people's help, I can't do anything. I've got to have you."

"There's no way that I'll jeopardize my job and my husband's
job," Maurine said. "I'll vote for the union, but that's as far as I'll
go."

Virginia Keyser did not take no for an answer. She came back
to visit several times. Finally she convinced Maurine to attend a

union meeting in Charlotte. It was a gathering of J. P. Stevens workers from plants all over the South.

At the meeting Maurine met other mill workers and was moved by their stories, so similar to those of mill workers in her own town. She met union leaders. One was Jim Pierce, who headed the organizing drive in Roanoke Rapids. Pierce asked Maurine to commit herself to the union cause, and Maurine explained her reluctance.

She told him, "I love Roanoke Rapids. It is my home, and I just don't want to leave it. If we became involved, not only me but my husband and everybody would all lose our jobs. I can't be part of getting other people involved because I won't be the cause of them losing their jobs too."

Pierce listened and then said, "Maurine, I'm not promising that you won't lose your job if you get involved. I'm hoping that won't happen, but it could. But I promise you that we'll never leave that town until you get your job back if it does happen. And that's a promise. Not just to you but to anybody else that gets involved."

"Well, fine," Maurine told him, and she believed Jim Pierce. She and a number of other workers returned to Roanoke Rapids convinced that the union was the only protection they had. Union officials had explained that it was illegal for the company to harass workers for union activities and that, if the company did violate their rights, it would be necessary to prove that management knew that these workers were union members. When the union sent a letter to J. P. Stevens with the names of Roanoke Rapids workers who had signed blue cards and were willing to have the company know it, Maurine's name was on the list.

"Right after that," Maurine said, "I went to sharpen my pencil at work one night. My bossman, William Johnson, the same one who had formed the Loom Fixers Club and asked me to sign a blue card five years before, came up to me.

" 'Maurine, are you campaigning for the union?'

" 'Not right now. I'm working for the company right now. But what I do after these eight hours is my business.'

" 'Well, I just didn't want you to get involved because there's two union men and one woman living over there in a motel that's using you people's money to shack up with.' "

Maurine told the union what Johnson had said to her. They had had similar reports of management's castigating the union. The cumulative instances of Stevens' harassment of union members were compiled and sent to the National Labor Relations Board. When the complaint came before the board, Maurine was asked to testify.

"I begged them—Hank Patterson, the board agent who took my statement, Jesse Butler, the attorney for the NLRB, everybody that I could see—to not make me do it. I knew that I was going out in just a little while for maternity leave. I *knew*, if I testified, that when I was out to have my baby the company would never take me back. I told Hank Patterson and Jesse Butler, 'I promise you before it's time for me to go back after my pregnancy leave, they'll get rid of my husband.' Patterson told me, 'Maurine, they'd never do it. That would be *too* obvious.' I said, 'You watch and see if what I'm telling you doesn't happen.'"

In August 1964 the National Labor Relations Board held hearings in Roanoke Rapids. Maurine told the Board what her boss had said to her. On August 29, 1964, nine days after she testified, Maurine left the mill on maternity leave. On October 17 she gave birth to a daughter, Deneen. That Christmas Eve, J. P. Stevens fired Doodle, allegedly for drinking on the job. Just after New Year's, when the baby was 2½ months old, Maurine reported back to work. She was told no jobs were available.

Twice a week, every Tuesday and Thursday, when the Rosemary Mill did its hiring, Maurine went to inquire about a job. Twice a week she was told no work was available.

While she was out of work, another union election was held. Maurine voted, but her vote was challenged because she was no longer at the mill. Once again the union was defeated. The TWUA got 1,186 votes; 1,684 voted against representation. The TWUA filed charges against Stevens, accusing the company of pre-election labor law violations. The NLRB substantiated the union claim and set aside the 1965 election.

With both Maurine and Doodle out of work and a young family to provide for, the Hedgepeth family had a hard time. Doodle could not find work. He was turned down everywhere he applied in town. He believes he was blacklisted. Finally he got a construction job in Hopewell, Virginia. He joined a carpool of other construction workers, including Clarence Brooks, Jr., and together they made the daily two-hundred-mile commute to their union jobs.

Maurine Hedgepeth was not alone in being harassed by the company for union activities. She was one of 289 workers from Stevens mills throughout the South who claimed in suits against the company that they had been illegally dismissed.

During the late sixties, fifteen suits involving these union adherents at Stevens mills dragged through the courts. Then Maurine's claim and one other were separated from the others filing suit with her; on January 31, 1967, trial examiner Boyd Leedom decided against Maurine and one other worker. In his finding he said of Maurine, "From my knowledge of her and her activity as revealed in the evidence, I conclude that insofar as union activity is concerned, she is the kind of person that Respondent would not have disturbed any more than the other union adherents who were not discharged."

On appeal to the NLRB, the Board reversed the administrative law judge and held that Maurine had indeed been fired for union-related reasons.

When the Stevens Company appealed the Board decision, the U. S. Court of Appeals for the Fourth Circuit upheld the Labor Board. The company was ordered to pay $1.3 million in cumulative back wages to all the workers who had been illegally discharged, including Maurine, and also to reinstate them.

Under the court order, Maurine and twenty-two others from the Roanoke Rapids mills were reinstated. Maurine had been out of work for four years and twenty-one days. During the years she was out of work, Jim Pierce remained true to his word that the union would stay in town until she got back her job.

"Virginia Keyser came here in 1963 and didn't leave until 1969," Maurine said. "I went back to work on a Friday, and on Sunday I went over to the union office and helped her pack up. When she left, she told me not to forget that the union was no farther away than a telephone call."

Returning was not easy for Maurine. "Six months went by before anyone spoke to me. The company had started a rumor that the $21,114 in back pay that the court made them pay me came out of the workers' pockets. When people believe you have taken money out of their pockets, they don't like it.

"I went back to prove that I wasn't wrong, that workers do have rights, that the company was going to have to work me whether they liked it or not. They would have liked nothing better than to have me quit," Maurine said. "But just because I was involved in the union and the company didn't want me back didn't mean that I was going to disappear or blow away."

PART SEVEN

He Ain't Hurting
No More

Retirement from J. P. Stevens

Since he had left the mill, Louis Harrell had spent much of his long-awaited retirement battling J. P. Stevens and its insurance carrier, Liberty Mutual Insurance Company, in his fight to win workers' compensation for brown lung.

He spent a lot of time, too, in and out of hospitals. Outside the room in the Halifax Memorial Hospital, the sign read: OXYGEN IN USE. Inside, Louis Harrell was alone, staring out the window, weak and sick. He had been out of the mill, on a leave of absence, for nine months.

"You know," Louis said, his voice barely a whisper, "the last day I was ever in the mill, June 16, 1976, was just a few weeks after I first talked with you. I had wanted so much to keep working until I reached retirement age. I would have had to keep working until this year, when I turn sixty-two to get early retirement, but I just couldn't make it.

"When I went back in to work that day, I wasn't feeling too good. I was still having trouble getting my breath. Most of the times before, I could make it all right at work by sneaking out and getting some air or just getting near an air conditioner for a few minutes. That last day, I just couldn't make it at all. They had to carry me out.

"After I left the mill, I went down to get my social security. They examined me down there. They run me through a pulmonary machine, the same like what we had at the brown lung clinic. They found enough wrong with me to say I was unable to work, and they give me my social security compensation. They never did say nothing about my brown lung. They told me I had heart trouble, which I knew, but they didn't say what my doctor did, that it was from the strain because of my lungs. Right now, I get $309 a month on social security disability. That's about two hundred dollars less than I'd make at the mill. But that's me and the taxpayers who puts into social security. That don't cost Stephenson nothing, having me collect from social security.

"Right now I'm on a leave of absence from the mill. What I have to do is wait till the year is up before I can tell the mill I'm retiring. If I told them now, all I'd get is what I would have if I had just quit for no reason. If I stay the year on disability, I'll get to take home twenty dollars a month in retirement.

"Now that's not much, but it's a whole heck of a lot better than I'd have gotten before the union come in. We don't have a contract yet, so the union's got to fight inch by inch, but there's been a lot of small improvements since the union come in.

"I can't get to first base with my workers' compensation. It's so slow. I told you the doctor already told me I had brown lung, but the way they've got it rigged up here in North Carolina, one of these ten doctors the state says is brown lung experts have to tell you you've got it before the mill's insurance company will give you your money.

"Guess who gets to pick which doctor you go to? The insurance company that's fighting you, that's who. You have to wait and wait until *they* decide to fix you up with an appointment."

Although it fights the claims of disabled workers with brown lung, Liberty Mutual Insurance Company has long been keenly aware of the dangers of cotton dust. The Boston-based company, which is the workers' compensation carrier for about seventy per cent of the textile industry, conducted extensive cotton-dust tests in its clients' mills at least as far back as 1968. Acting as a safety inspector as a service to its textile customers, Liberty Mutual took 1,388 air samples in 1973 and an additional 400 samples in thirty-three mills in 1976. Liberty Mutual has done an overall survey of cotton dust in J. P. Stevens mills. Many of the samples provided proof of dangerously high cotton-dust levels in the mills.

Melvin B. Bradshaw, the president of Liberty Mutual, saw no

reason to inform the workers his company supposedly was protecting that they were exposed to hazardous levels of cotton dust.

"I don't believe it is our prerogative to give employees this information. We do this work strictly as a consultant to the company." Bradshaw added, "If they are working in the mills, they must know it's dangerous."

Although 400,000 American workers develop occupational diseases each year, and 100,000 die annually as a result of these diseases, not more than five hundred cases a year are compensated through the workers' compensation system. Half of the deaths are due to lung diseases such as byssinosis and cancer. The insurance companies contest 88 per cent of all dust-disease cases that result in awards.

The reason Liberty Mutual fought so hard was that the average cost of occupational-disease cases is fifty per cent higher than the average for occupational-accident cases. The number of workers involved is high: According to a recent study by the pioneering byssinosis researcher Dr. Arend Bouhuys, 35,000 workers have suffered disabling lung damage as a result of exposure to cotton dust.

Louis Harrell pulled himself up in his hospital bed. "That Liberty Mutual that Stephenson's got, they've stalled me and stalled me. They finally gave me an appointment with a doctor a hundred miles away. After I had already left home that morning to go over, they called my house. Do you know what they wanted to say? They'd canceled my appointment. Can you beat that?

"Well, I finally got another appointment out of them. It was over in Durham at the Duke University Medical Center. Charlotte Brody, from over at the brown lung office, went with me. We were walking from the parking lot to the hospital, and I started to get short of breath. I was real bad off. That Charlotte, she's a registered nurse. She tried to help me, but I couldn't make it. My heart just gave out from straining to pump oxygen to my lungs. I had a heart attack right there on the steps of the hospital.

"So they carried me into the hospital for that. I didn't have the strength for all those breathing tests they give you to see if you have brown lung, so I never did get my lungs tested that time. Now Liberty Mutual is saying they'll get me another appointment when I'm well enough to go again.

"I've been trying so hard to stay out of the hospital, but I've had several heart attacks and my breathing just gets worse and worse. They had to carry me in on Christmas Day and on New Year's Day too. In the last three months I've been in the hospital three times."

As we talked, Lillian Harrell came in with news of the family. The couple was awaiting the birth of a grandchild. After a while Lillian turned up the sound of the television set that had been on. "Sixty Minutes" was airing an exposé on occupational health hazards, and Dan Rather was interviewing employees of the Velsicol Chemical Company, based in Chicago. The firm produced Phosvel, a pesticide that was banned from the U.S. market. Rather said that the company was exporting it to Egypt.

"What are they selling it to Egypt for?" Lillian asked. "To kill their people with?"

Louis listened to Velsicol workers tell Dan Rather that they had become like "zombies" after being exposed to Phosvel. Rather said that the company's annual report did not discuss what happened to its workers who had been exposed to Phosvel except to call it "a regrettable industrial accident."

Lillian and Louis watched as three Velsicol supervisors blamed the plant manager for allowing the occupational hazard. Rather asked the men why they didn't file a complaint with the Department of Labor's Occupational Safety and Health Administration.

"Because they were scared to lose their jobs and all that good money," Lillian said.

"That OSHA," Louis said, his head propped up with pillows, "they take their time inspecting, and when they do go in and catch them, they put a fine on them of six or eight dollars."

Toward the end of the "Sixty Minutes" program, Mike Wallace reviewed the letters and comments on an earlier program about J. P. Stevens and the union struggle in Roanoke Rapids. He said, "Two weeks ago, in our story on the struggle between the AFL-CIO and the J. P. Stevens Company, we were in error on one point and our report was incomplete. We said that the average Stevens worker makes $3.65 an hour. That was wrong. Stevens says the correct figure, including overtime, is $3.98 an hour. We also reported that Stevens workers are limited to one week of vacation, regardless of length of service. That is correct. But we should also have reported that after five years, Stevens workers are entitled to two weeks of vacation pay, and three weeks of vacation pay after fifteen years, though they can't take more than a week off."

Lillian listened to Mike Wallace. "I never did hear tell of that. After thirty years, we're still getting the same thing. We don't get no three weeks' pay. J.P. is a dirty liar."

"Finally," Mike Wallace said, "there has been one new development. Last week, in a rare action, the National Labor Relations Board itself took Stevens to court, charging the company with failing to bargain in good faith with the union at its plants in Roanoke Rapids, North Carolina, where the union won recognition over two years ago."

Hearing this, Louis smiled and clapped his hands together over his big chest. When he was still active, he had been a strong union member.

In the year after he left the mill, Louis Harrell's health deteriorated rapidly. Two years after he left the mill, one year and one day after he was officially retired, Louis had yet another breathing attack. That one was fatal. The day he died, his grief-stricken daughter, who had tried so hard to get him to leave the mill before he was totally disabled, said, "At least he ain't hurting no more."

Louis Harrell was buried on his forty-first wedding anniversary. He had worn a suit and tie the day that he and Lillian married. But Louis, who had had so much difficulty breathing in the last years of his life, could not stand the thought of a necktie constricting his throat. He requested that he be buried without one.

At his funeral, the Roanoke Rapids chapter of the Carolina Brown Lung Association filed past the casket of their fallen brother. Just before his casket was closed, Louis's friend and fellow CBLA officer Ola Harrell pinned a "Cotton Dust Kills" button on Louis's lapel.

The minister stood behind Louis's casket and said, "We are here today to honor Louis Harrell and to find strength for our grief. We are grateful for all our happy moments with him. We are grateful for all the noble deeds that have been accomplished by Louis."

Then the minister prayed, "Father, in the days ahead, let us not dwell on what might have been. And let us thank you for letting Louis Harrell be the inspiration and the teacher that he was."

After the service, the funeral cortege wended through the streets of Roanoke Rapids, where the Harrell family had woven and spun, lived and died, since the town was started. Family, friends, and members of the Carolina Brown Lung Association mournfully followed Louis's body on its last trip past the mills. At the New Mill, where Louis had worked, three women stood at the window, solemnly watching the procession go by. Then the cortege passed the Rosemary Mill and the Patterson Mill.

As Louis was being buried, in Washington the Department of Labor was announcing the promulgation of a cotton-dust standard that allowed the textile industry an additional four years to reduce the levels of cotton dust in the mills.

The Amalgamated Clothing and Textile Workers Union filed suit in the U. S. Court of Appeals in Washington, asserting that the new standard would fail to protect the health of workers, and the American Textile Manufacturers Institute went to the federal appeals court in Richmond, Virginia, in an attempt to block the new regulation, saying it was highly inflationary and technologically impossible to meet in some parts of the mills.

In Raleigh other chapters of the Carolina Brown Lung Association met with reporters to express their dismay with the standard which they felt was too weak and which, they told the press, was too late for mill workers like Louis Harrell.

The North Carolina Industrial Commission, also in Raleigh, unaware that Louis Harrell had died, prepared a letter informing him that he had been denied all compensation for his lungs.

After Louis's family and friends had left the grave site, a funeral home employee rearranged the wreaths on the grave. A cemetery caretaker stood nearby. The funeral agent fingered the ribbon on the wreath donated by the Carolina Brown Lung Association. "Cotton Dust Kills," he said. "Baloney. Cancer kills, knives kill, people kill."

When he had walked away, the black caretaker muttered under his breath, "And the mills kill." He had worked in textiles himself. "When you get a job around here, it has to be awful bad not to stick with it, but I couldn't take the mill.

"The company gives you all this razzmatazzmatazz, and you can't do anything about it. I would have stuck with the mill if there had been a union. If the company didn't rule your life, it could be a pretty good job." He took a last, sad look at Louis Harrell's fresh grave and walked away.

Sunday. Wanda, daughter of Ernestine and Clarence Brooks, Jr.

Which side are you on?

New York. Corporate headquarters for the second largest U.S. textile firm.

Roanoke Rapids. A court record of bad-faith bargaining with the union negotiating team.

Roanoke Rapids looking toward a better day.

Roanoke Rapids. A court record of bad-faith bargaining with the union negotiating team.

Roanoke Rapids looking toward a better day.

Rise gonna rise.

PART EIGHT

A New Day

Seeking Justice
in an Unjust Society

Instead of thousands of anti-Stevens demonstrators thronging the streets outside the Stevens Tower in New York, on March 7, 1978, two dozen white pro-company supporters stood just inside the entrance to the fenced-in parking lot surrounding the fortresslike Textile Hall on Exposition Avenue in Greenville, South Carolina. Not wanting a repeat of the 1977 shareholders meeting, J. P. Stevens had moved its annual meeting to Greenville, an antiunion bastion and corporate base for Stevens' southern operation.

A hand-painted wooden sign atop a station wagon parked nearby the paltry picket line read: "Please Help Me Keep the Union Out of the Textile Plants in the South by Supporting Free Enterprise." Few of the cars turning in stopped to take the leaflet entitled "Free Enterprise and Against Boycotting" that W. C. Galloway, Sr., a retired Stevens supervisor from Greenville, was handing out. Mildred Ramsey, a weaver from Greenville, identified by the others as a leader of the group, said the demonstrators were members of "Stevens People and Friends for Freedom." "We're a sister organization to the J. P. Stevens Employees Educational Committee they've got up in Roanoke Rapids," she said.

Gene Patterson in dark sunglasses and a T-shirt reading, "JPSEEC Oust the Union," said, "The Educational Committee is paying all my expenses here. Me and Mr. Bob Click, our consultant, flew down here yesterday from Roanoke Rapids. We'll be flying back together this afternoon."

The pro-company demonstrators, warming themselves against the cold in "Stand Up for J. P. Stevens" shirts, said they would like to be inside the meeting instead of outside in the parking lot. "Maybe next year we will be," one of them said wistfully.

Some 250 Stevens workers, who had taken the day off without pay and driven hundreds of miles to Greenville, had already gone into the cavernous Textile Hall. Ironically, these workers were a contingent of ACTWU members from Roanoke Rapids and workers from Stevens mills all over the South who had signed union cards.

They passed the signs at the entrance demanding that cameras and tape recording equipment be checked, walked into the meeting, and faced James Finley. He stood on a stage four feet in the air, behind a lectern and a row of potted palms, beyond the cordon of top executives and board wives. Even here he could not escape the strength of Stevens workers.

They did not take their eyes off him as he told the shareholders, "The Amalgamated Clothing and Textile Workers Union continues its boycott and massive propaganda campaign in an avowed effort to organize our employees and discredit the good name of our company. The incontestable proof of the failure of the boycott lies in the fact that our sales and profits have not been affected by their efforts."

Then they heard him say, "Nineteen seventy-seven profits did not meet our expectations, and for the 1978 first quarter, net income fell seven per cent." Finley added, "The company's employees are enthusiastic. Barring some major economic calamity not discernible at this time, we face 1978 in a generally optimistic state of mind."

James Boone and Maurine Hedgepeth, Lucy Taylor and Otis Edwards listened as the board chairman said, "The union's organizing campaign has been accompanied since June 1976 by an AFL-CIO boycott of the company which is unparalleled in U.S. business history in its magnitude, scope, and intensity. Management believes that the implementation of its concern for the interest of the employees, and its resistance to the union's organiz-

ing campaigns and the accompanying AFL-CIO boycott, have
been beneficial to the company."

When Finley had finished his prepared statement, wave after
wave of Stevens workers stood to demand that the wrongs done to
them be righted. And a proposal was made to add minority
representatives to the Stevens board of directors. James Finley
told the shareholders that the company had been unable to find a
woman to serve on its board. "We were turned down twice by two
women who said they did not want to serve on our board as long
as we had these activists working against this company."

Bob Hall of Chapel Hill, North Carolina, the editor of *Southern Exposure* magazine, shot back at Finley, "Your board is composed of all men, entirely white, as white as the cotton dust in
your mills. It's time for the Stevens board to come into the twentieth century. I'm not at all surprised that the two women you
approached to be on your board turned you down. Like many of
your other friends, they don't want to take a position of being
associated openly with you."

Two people who had worked for Stevens were nominated from
the floor to represent minorities on the board. Lucy Taylor was
one, and the other was Addie Jackson, a black woman from the
Statesboro, Georgia, plant that Stevens shut down. She said to
Finley, "It's high time that you wake up and find out what is going
on. The only way you are going to find out is to have someone
up there who knows what is going on."

More Stevens workers stood to air grievances. Varnell Coates, a
member of the Roanoke Rapids chapter of the CBLA, told Finley,
"I worked for J. P. Stevens for thirty-five years. For all those years
of work, all I get in retirement is twenty dollars a month. That
only comes to $240 a year. You, Mr. Finley, will get $90,000 a year
in retirement when you leave. To me, Mr. Finley, and to the employees who work for J. P. Stevens, this is not fair."

In a pale attempt to identify himself with the workers, to blur
the distinction between management and labor, Finley told the
meeting that he himself had worked in the mills, that he had just
been "lucky" to work his way up to the top position.

Lucy Taylor stepped to the microphone. "Did you get brown
lung working in the mills?" she asked.

Finley, startled, responded, "I don't know."

"Well, I heard you coughing before. I think you might have it."

"Could be," the chairman said.

A worker from Stevens' Estes Plant near Greenville addressed the meeting. "In my plant we're working on shifts, A, B, C, and D. We're off every other weekend. We do fifty-six hours' labor for about forty-two hours' pay. We work twelve-hour shifts. You can't even go to church on Sunday when you have to work twelve hours a day. They fired a preacher here who worked for them for twenty-six years because he wanted to get off work to preach on Sunday. This is called a fair labor practice? No. And the company—"

Finley interrupted him and told the man to state his grievances to his supervisor.

"I already did, and I got the same answers from him as I get from you. No answer."

Bob Hall offered a shareholder proposal for a special report on the impact of the company's labor-management policies on the economic performance of the company's stock. Hall's statement was printed in Stevens' proxy statement: "Much evidence indicates that Stevens' stock performance may be affected by its policies toward labor unions. For example, on August 31, 1977, the Second Circuit Court of Appeals opened the way for the company to receive stiff fines if it continues violating the labor-management laws and the Court's orders. The following week, Stevens stock fell from sixteen and seven-eighths to five and seven-eighths while other textile stocks remained relatively unchanged.

"In fact by October 19, J. P. Stevens stock price was thirteen per cent below its low price for 1976. Stevens stock has performed worse than any of the other leading textile companies. At least one investment consultant has attributed the poor performance to Stevens' labor-management problems."

Hall addressed Finley, "*The Gallagher Presidents' Report, A Confidential Letter to Chief Executives,* names you, Mr. Finley, as one of the ten worst chief executives for 1977 for 'outdated labor practices resulting in contempt of court citation, for effort by the National Labor Relations Board to obtain a nationwide injunction against the company, for a union boycott of the company's products.'

"I would like to see the price of Stevens stock go up, Mr.

Finley. J. P. Stevens has become the rotten apple of Wall Street. It is viewed as the rotten apple by the textile industry."

James Finley shifted his weight and looked distinctly uncomfortable. At the end of the meeting, he stepped down from the dais and walked over to the press tables. The press corps asked Finley about the rumors that he would be leaving the board of New York's Manufacturers Hanover Trust Company, the holding company for the bank of the same name.

For over a year, it had been the target of an ACTWU campaign because more than $1 billion in union trust and pension funds were deposited with the bank which had an avowed antiunionist on its board. ACTWU's strategy was either to force corporate responsiveness from Manufacturers Hanover or to isolate J. P. Stevens from its financial ties.

Answering the reporters' questions, Finley replied, "I have decided that I will not stand for re-election to the board. To be quite honest, the bank put enough pressure on me that I decided against seeking re-election. I don't want to be where I am not wanted."

The night before they faced down the chairman of the board, 250 Stevens workers from southern towns dominated by the mill company gathered in a Greenville motel to present their own human rights annual report. James Finley was not there as Stevens employees from Montgomery, Alabama, who had been fired for union activity; Statesboro, Georgia, workers, out of work for three years; and Roanoke Rapids workers, on the front line, fighting for a contract for three years, joined together.

These women and men, young and old, black and white, healthy and ill, who had been kept apart by the giant corporate power which tried to control their lives, took charge of their own meeting.

Union members, organizers, and officials; brown lung victims; and workers fired for supporting the union sat together underneath eight poster-sized photographs of Stevens workers—the union heroines and heroes—people like those in this room who had put their lives, their jobs, and their beliefs on the line.

Reverend Edward Fleming stood and said, "Let us pray. We

ask Thee to be with us, and we ask Thee to direct our activities today. We come seeking justice in this unjust society."

When the prayer was finished, Reverend Fleming said, "At stake is taking a stand on an issue facing us as a people today. We find Moses was the first person who became conscious of his people who were in slavery. They had been captivated by a people who were using their labor without due reward. We too can do no less than face the issue.

"I am the pastor of four churches. Many of the members of my congregation are members of this company. And I myself worked for J. P. Stevens." Reverend Fleming bit off the end of the word, "Stevens," in a conscious adjustment of his pronunciation since James Finley told him the company was not "Stephenson." "I worked for Stevens for twenty-three years in the yarn and dye plant. People ask me, 'What's it like to be a J. P. Stevens worker?' I know what it's like to be fired out of your job for preaching the Gospel.

"At our meeting tonight we will give a J. P. Stevens annual report on human conditions, not sales and not income. We will talk about the losses in human terms. The difference between the J. P. Stevens annual report and ours is the difference between profits and human beings."

Shouts of "All right!" and "Amen, brother!" came from the Stevens workers.

"Which comes first, profits or human beings?" Fleming asked.

"Human beings!" the Stevens workers shouted back.

"That's right," the preacher said with a smile, acknowledging the spirit in the gathering. "J. P. Stevens says they've changed. They say they have been born again, if you know what I'm talking about."

The people laughed and applauded. "We know! We know!"

"Our report is going to show that unless you and I change them, Stevens is like a tiger. It can't change its stripes."

"Tell it like it is!"

"All of us have been Stevens workers. We have come here from six states to speak for ourselves."

Maurine Hedgepeth, James Boone, Otis Edwards, Lucy Taylor, Cecil Jones, and Clyde Bush listened as Bennett Taylor, a union member from Roanoke Rapids spoke. "I work in Stevens' Fabricating Plant. If I had been working for Stevens thirty years ago, I'd be sweeping up, cleaning up, hauling coal." Otis Edwards, listening to the younger black man, nodded his head in silent agreement.

"Stevens says they have 23 per cent that belong to minority groups. What they fail to say is what category of jobs these minorities are in.

"The case known as *Sledge* v. *J. P. Stevens* shows this discrimination better than anything else. I know because I worked with Lucy Sledge." Then Bennett Taylor told the Stevens workers from other mill towns what happened to Lucy Sledge, sharing her story, their history.

Lucy Taylor addressed the gathering. Over her head was a photograph of Louis Harrell. Lucy explained the CBLA to the Stevens workers who did not yet have chapters. "We are a tight organization. We love each other. We cry when one of us dies, and we've had several of us die. We have to be up there visiting in the hospital. Sometimes I'm up there all taped up, all oxygened up.

"Thirty-five thousand mill workers have brown lung. These are not numbers. These are *crimes* that cause injury and death just as sure as if they took a gun to us.

"When Stevens workers organize themselves together in a union, together we can make the mill a place we are proud to work in. We can see the time that we are going to make Stevens' empty promises into a union reality."

Just before the close of the worker meeting, Reverend Fleming said, "There has always been a Moses that comes to the rescue of his people. We could not have done what we have done, accomplished what we will accomplish, without the union organizers and union officials and union lawyers who have worked so hard for us."

Reverend Fleming introduced Sol Stetin, senior executive vice-president of ACTWU. Stetin talked to the workers about the "epic campaign" that they were all part of. The workers from Stevens' chain of mills—that snake through the Carolinas and arc into Tennessee, Alabama, and Georgia—cheered for their own hard work and their role in the struggle to create more human bonds between themselves, links forged for a new life, a new kind of union.

As Stetin said, "I promise you that one day there will be a victory celebration," all the J. P. Stevens workers rose to their feet and clapped and shouted for joy. Then slowly the mood changed, and the workers, as if bound by a single spirit, linked hands and sang chorus after chorus of "We Shall Overcome."

LIST OF PHOTOGRAPHS

Following page 12.
Hattie Baker, Lincoln Heights.
J. P. Stevens River Mill, Roanoke Rapids.
J. P. Stevens Rosemary Mill, Roanoke Rapids.
Cotton-mill worker, Ware Shoals, South Carolina.
Otis Edwards, Carmen Harrison, and Kasper Smith, Roanoke Rapids.
Louis Harrell with his grandson Edward Harrell.
Kasper Smith with his granddaughter Charlene Smith, Halifax County.
Maurine Hedgepeth and James Boone at the union hall, Roanoke Rapids.

Following page 36.
Ben Fleming, Hodgestown.
Residents of Weldon.
Eula and Frankie Wood, Roanoke Rapids.
First Baptist Church, Halifax.
Masonic Lodge, Enfield.
Boys from Prince Street, Hodgestown.
Housing, Lincoln Heights.
Housing, Weldon.
"Big Jim" Jones, Northampton County.

MIMI CONWAY is an investigative reporter who has concentrated on the southern textile industry and occupational health since 1975. Her work on brown lung disease has been called the "only . . . truly investigative piece of journalism" on the subject by the *Columbia Journalism Review*. In 1976 she received a grant from the Fund for Investigative Journalism to do research on the textile industry. She wrote for *Newsweek* from Hong Kong, where she lived from 1968 to 1971, and her freelance articles have appeared in *Newsday*, *Esquire*, the Washington *Post*, the *Progressive*, the New York *Times*, the *Village Voice*, the St. Petersburg *Times*, and other publications.

EARL DOTTER is a photojournalist specializing in labor subjects. Health and safety on the job has been a recurring theme in his workplace photography of coal miners, auto workers, and textile workers. Mr. Dotter was the staff photographer for the *United Mine Workers Journal* from 1973 through 1977. His exhibit "In Our Blood: Coal Miners in the Seventies" was considered by the New York *Times* one of the ten most important photographic events of 1977. His pictures of textile workers are slated for exhibition in 1979.

INDEX